RACQUETBALL strategy

JEAN SAUSER AND ARTHUR SHAY

Contemporary Books, Inc.
Chicago

Library of Congress Cataloging in Publication Data

Sauser, Jean.
    Racquetball strategy.

    Includes index.
    1. Racquetball.   I. Shay, Arthur, joint
author.   II. Title.
GV1017.R3S287   1979   796.34'3   78-73676
ISBN 0-8092-7366-7
ISBN 0-8092-7365-9 pbk.

Copyright © 1979 by Jean Sauser and Arthur Shay
All rights reserved
Published by Contemporary Books, Inc.
180 North Michigan Avenue, Chicago, Illinois 60601
Manufactured in the United States of America
Library of Congress Catalog Card Number: 78-73676
International Standard Book Number: 0-8092-7366-7 (cloth)
                                                  0-8092-7365-9 (paper)
Published simultaneously in Canada by
Beaverbooks
953 Dillingham Road
Pickering, Ontario L1W 1Z7
Canada

Contents

v	Acknowledgments	26	Playing a player who covers most of the court with his backhand
vii	Introduction		
1	Male about to play a female	27	You've given your opponent a set-up off the back wall
2	Female about to play a male	28	Your opponent has given you a set-up off the back wall
3	Playing an out-of-shape opponent		
4	Playing when you're out of shape	31	You've given your opponent a front wall/back wall set-up
5	Playing an older player		
6	Playing a younger player	32	Your opponent gives you a front wall/back wall set-up
7	Playing with a fast ball		
8	Playing with a slow ball	36	You are forced to hit the ball into the back wall
9	Your opponent hits the ball very hard		
10	Your opponent hits the ball softly	38	Your opponent has slammed the ball into the back wall
11	Playing a player who covers most of the court with his forehand	39	Receiving during the first ten points of the game
12	Your opponent crowds you	40	Serving in the first half of the game
14	You crowd your opponent	44	You have only one serve attempt left
16	Your opponent watches the front wall	47	You are serving and winning the game
18	You watch the front wall	48	Receiving garbage or lob serves
20	You've won the first serve	50	Receiving and your opponent is ahead
22	You are receiving the first serve	51	Serving the game point

52	Your opponent is serving the game point	64	Your opponent hits an overhead smash to the corner
53	Intercepting a cross-court pass to your forehand	65	You are trapped at a side wall
54	Your opponent has intercepted your cross-court pass to his forehand	66	Your opponent is trapped at a side wall
55	Cutting off a down-the-line shot to your backhand	68	Your opponent has dived to retrieve the ball
56	Your opponent is cutting off your down-the-line shot	70	You have dived to retrieve the ball
57	Your opponent is chasing your pass shot around the backhand corner with his forehand	73	Opponents' right side player is too close to the right wall
58	You've chased a cross-court pass around your backhand corner	74	Your right side player is too close to the right wall
59	Returning the corner kill	76	It's the first time you've played doubles with your partner
60	Your opponent returns your corner kill	78	Returning the forehand corner kill
61	You have a set-up in center court	79	Returning the Z ball
62	Your opponent has a set-up in center court	80	The forehand set-up
63	Your opponent is anticipating a ceiling shot	82	Your opponents have a set-up
		83	Glossary
		87	Index

Acknowledgments

We would like to thank the Northbrook and Highland Park, Illinois, Sky Harbor Clubs for the use of their courts for some of the photographs in this book. Also the Evergreen Park Bath and Tennis Club, and Steve Shay for some of the pictures he took there. Thanks are also due to pros Marty Hogan, Charlie Brumfield, Jerry Hilecher, Janelle Marriott, Kathy Williams, and to semi-pro Bill Brin for his valuable suggestions. Warm appreciation is felt for the numerous models—real live A and B players who contributed their time and court energy. Some of the better action shots were taken by Steve Shay, 19.

Special thanks to Charlie Drake of Leach Industries, Bob Kendler and Chuck Leve of the National Racquetball Association for their help and permission to use some of the pictures shot on the pro tour, including the cover, which was shot during the Nationals at the Sports Illustrated Court Club near Detroit.

The cover shows the two greatest racquetball players who ever lived, Charlie Brumfield and Marty Hogan, trying to outdo each other.

Introduction

Now that there are about ten million racquetball players of varying skills, the number of "intermediate" players—C players determined to become Bs and B players determined to become As—has increased proportionately.

While locker room talk used to focus on the execution of shots, the emphasis these days is on strategy.

"I had him in the deep backhand corner and instead of hitting it up front off the side wall, I blasted it and the ball came right back to him."

"She was way out of position, cowering against the side wall, and instead of shooting the ball right past her for a pinch, I . . ."

One of the delights of my sometime occupation as chief photographer and writer for *National Racquetball* magazine is being privy to the after-game conversations with pros such as Marty Hogan, Charlie Brumfield, Steve Strandemo, Peggy Steding, Shannon Wright, and the rest of the superstars.

"If I hadn't dived," Hilecher said to Benny Koltun, "I would've never caught up to the ball at the back wall."

"And I would've won the match," replied Koltun sadly.

"I could feel Marty missing his forehand kills by two inches—that's a lot," said Brumfield after the recent Nationals (see cover). "But I couldn't take advantage of him; he's so fast."

Charlie Drake, Marty Hogan's guru and the head of Leach Industries (and a former pro himself), says of Hogan, "His sense of strategy reminds me of the jungle animal cornered. I mean Hogan always plays strategically as if he's about to be ambushed."

"And that's the way I like Charlie Brumfield to play Hogan," adds Carl Loveday, a Golden Masters champion and Brumfield's coach. "Like he has the kid cornered and must choose the best percentage shot every time. And, when on the defensive, as if he himself is cornered. All these pros respond to their own desperation."

One of the master court strategists, U.S. Racquetball Association founder and President Bob Kendler, says, "The best racquetball players have all learned their strategy from handball, where you find out an opponent's weakness and work on it with the best shot you've got for every strategic situation."

U.S. Racquetball Association official Dan Bertolucci says, "After the first year of play, a racquetball player naturally wants to move up in class and achievement. The most room for improvement lies in strategy. Of course you learn to improve your basic arsenal of shots while working on strategy, but the smarts you get from strategy are the real ladder to improving your racquetball. I used to hit hard but indiscriminately. Playing with pros like Terry Fancher, John Lynch, and Marty Hogan—not to sound egotistical—have smartened my play."

A 38-year-old Chicago businessman, Bill Brin, had become an A player two years ago. "But I didn't start winning those Saturday morning club tournaments," he said recently, "until Jean Sauser gave me a dozen lessons in racquetball strategy."

So here are those dozen lessons and a few more! Be strategic and win!

Arthur Shay

Situation: You're male and are about to play a female.

It is often intimidating for a man to enter a club's B tournament and discover his first round opponent is a woman. The instant pressure—perhaps rising from the possibility of losing to a woman in public—can easily handicap you five points. If you're a gentleman by most standards and have grown up to "the weaker sex," you may start thinking, "I'll win, but not by too much." This kind of thinking leads to disaster.

Strategy: Use power

The advantage you have, generally speaking, is power. Most males are simply more powerful than most women.

So use this power to overpower your female opponent. Serve hard drive serves, hard Z serves. Don't get into pitty-pat rallies and other time-consuming defensive maneuvers. Shoot the right shot at the right time as hard as you can, still keeping control of the ball.

Recent studies have shown that the power superiority of males over females is fairly universal, but equally universal is the superiority of female endurance when it has been developed by practice and conditioning.

Using your power edge against female players will inevitably help you develop a formidable weapon for use against other males with varying degrees of power. "Power racquetball" is the game's latest direction. It works for Marty Hogan and other hard hitters. Make it work for you.

1

Situation: You're female and are about to play a male.

You're about to play a male of untested skills on the court. Or you're a pretty good player and have entered the men's division tournament or ladder to get better racquetball competition.

You have several psychological advantages going for you. First, you're generally the underdog. Second, your male opponent will tighten up because he will be trying especially hard not to be beaten by a woman. This kind of defeat is harder for a male to accept than a female. There are lots of points in exploiting this tightness.

Strategy: Play position

Position on the court is one of the most crucial weapons for the female under court attack by a male. Try to use ceiling balls or deep court pass shots to keep your opponent behind you. These shots will keep him off balance in the back court. Thought can overcome power in many situations, so think. Be the gazelle against the lion. Use speed and position against all that intimidating power.

On the pro tour, veteran strategist Charlie Brumfield often takes a game or two from powerhouse Marty Hogan by outmaneuvering him. (See cover.)

Expect your male opponent to try the power game, usually his best weapon. Refuse to be intimidated by a few points lost to blinding serves. Make sure your body is in a good position—generally facing one side wall or the other—before you swing at the serve. Get set this way as fast as you can. Most men can't control their power too well and their hard shots end up going to the back wall high and caroming back down the court off a side wall for what the pros call "a plum"—an easy shot to put away. Bide your time and get set for

these plums, then track these balls down and put them into a front corner—preferably side wall to front wall for an unpredictable pinch shot. (A pinch can be side wall-front wall or front wall-side wall.) The crazy angle at which the ball comes out will work for you.

Situation: Playing an out-of-shape opponent.

Strategy: Pass and pinch

If you're in reasonably good shape and are up against a blubbery, hard-breathing foe who seems to be dying after every rally, take advantage of the blubber and the shortness of breath. Keep the ball away from your opponent, moving it around him with pass shots. Alternate pass shots with side wall-front wall pinch shots. Get the ball into play quickly on serves. Alternate your serves, getting them as far from your opponent as possible.

Situation: Playing when you're out of shape.

Strategy: Hold center court position and shoot the ball

Besides taking a firm vow that you will never let yourself get out of shape again, grit your teeth, tighten your lips, and get a very slightly increased bend into your stance as you get set.

When you're playing an opponent who is in better shape than you, try to keep him/her behind you with deep passing shots. Try to force your opponent into making errors by hitting hard when you have a clear shot at the ball and the time to get into good position.

Use the center court position, a circle about six feet in diameter starting about two feet in back of the short line, as a home away from home on the court. Some strategists eschew the use of this position, but hanging around center court will make it possible for you to get the most coverage for the least number of enervating steps. This is a must if you're really out of shape and breathing hard after every rally. (Obviously, you should be cautioned against going on the court at all without a doctor's OK if you're *really* out of shape.)

You should serve with as much power as you can muster, and use those corner pinches, if you can manage them, to cut down the length of rallies that will quickly fatigue you in your run-down condition.

Use your time-outs toward the end of the game, or after long volleys that use up your wind.

Jogging and swimming are the best and fastest conditioners for racquetball. Jogging half a mile a day three times a week is a good way to start.

Situation: Playing an older player.

Some of the most deadly accurate players look as if they came from your parents' alumni association. They creak and complain and brush back what's left of their gray hair and then get on the court and run you into the ground. In few sports does experience teach as much as it does in racquetball. That aging mental computer has experienced just about every shot and every court position, and knows how to deal with it while expending a minimum of energy.

Strategy: Play smart

It therefore becomes your job to outsmart the senior. You must learn to choose high percentage shots—rather than try off-balance kills. You must constantly try to keep your older opponent on the move toward the rear wall and back front again. Pinch shots should be used to work against the possibly fading reflexes of a good front court player. That is, take advantage of that split-second lag some older players have in diagnosing a fast shot and getting to it in time.

Many older players develop accurate soft and slow shots to the front wall. Be prepared at all times to charge forward and backward to retrieve these possible plums. Use power when you can.

A good rule of thumb is to kill when you're in front of an older player and pass when you are behind him.

Situation: Playing a younger player.

Strategy: Play position

Keep control of center court and move him or her around you with passes and ceiling shots. Find out what he can and can't do. If you drive the ball into the deep corners of the court you may force errors, if he is an inexperienced player, because he will probably try to shoot the ball from all over, trying difficult kills—and it will be easier for you to capitalize on his mistakes. Vary your serves; alternate fast and slow serves. The slow serves may tempt your opponent into kill shots that often miss, or may give you an easy set-up return.

Situation: Playing with a fast ball.

There are two types of racquetballs, pressurized and nonpressurized. Balls that come in pressurized cans are usually faster and require a different game style than balls that are not pressurized. To see what kind of ball you are playing with—fast or slow—hit a medium-speed ceiling shot. If it travels with snap and bounces high to the back wall, you are playing with a fast ball.

Strategy: Hit lower and harder

To play your best with a fast ball and be able to control it you will have to change your shots slightly. Play a faster, lower power game. Pass shots will have to be hit lower than the normal two feet off the floor. Hitting that front wall only one foot off the floor, and sometimes even lower, will now make a good pass shot. High lob serves are out. A lob serve with a live ball will almost always come off the back wall for a "plum" shot for your opponent. Your ceiling shots will have to be hit softer, again to prevent that back wall set-up. Generally, when you shoot a fast ball, aim low. Corner shots, especially, must be accurate kills, or they will pop into center court for a set-up. The key to playing a fast ball is to hit it as low as possible, hard, and with a good angle.

If you have a choice, choose a fast ball when you're playing a fast, hard-hitting player who has little control of his shots. You will retrieve more deep court shots than you could with a slower ball that dies up front.

The two all-time-best racquetball players, Charlie Brumfield and Marty Hogan, playing with a fast ball.

Situation: Playing with a slow ball.

A slow ball throws off everyone's timing, but by learning to adapt—for example, by hitting ceiling shots harder—you can gain an edge.

Balls that do not come in pressurized cans but in boxes or nonpressurized cans are usually slower. To test for a slow ball, hit a medium-speed ceiling shot. If the ball fails to bounce higher than your head, you have a slow ball. Bouncing two or three balls comparatively should help weed out the real clunkers.

Strategy: Play a control game

The slow ball lends itself to a control or defensive game. Hit your ceiling shots slightly harder than normal, so that they do not fall short of deep court. Your pass shots will have to be higher—two or three feet above the floor at the front wall—so that the ball will carry to deep court and not bounce up short in front court for a set-up. Serves can be lobs or "garbage serves," soft, deep serves to your opponent's weaker side, which lend themselves very well to a slower ball. Drive serves can be effective, but you will have to hit them harder or higher on the front wall to get them in. Be careful not to fatigue yourself trying to blast drive serves with a slow ball. Changes in speed can be effective in a game with a slow ball.

Situation: Your opponent hits the ball very hard.

Strategy: Slow the game down

Before the match begins, get the slowest, lowest-bouncing ball that he will agree to play with. To try and play a hard-hitting opponent who can control his shots with a lively ball will make it harder for you to react to his cannon shots. The first thing to try in mid-game is to slow up the pace with well-executed ceiling shots. Power hitters are notorious for having no patience with ceiling balls, trying to shoot them for low kills at every chance, and because they often miss the kill, leaving set-ups for you in mid-court or off the back wall. Play an aggressor aggressively. Hit your passes and kills hard, deliberately, sharply, and cleanly. If you can't overpower him, emulate him.

Situation: Your opponent hits the ball softly with a lot of finesse.

Strategy: Play a faster pace

Blow the ball by her with every opportunity, using as much power as you can muster. Hit hard, fast pass shots. To leave a finesse player—one who consistently makes good shots—in center court is deadly. Run her around as much as possible, because a finesse player must usually stop to hit in order to play her best. If you can keep a player like this on the run, you'll find her finesse turns into set-ups for you to put away. Stay away from ceiling rallies because this type of player will be more patient than you and unjustly likes to volley for a long time before trying for a kill.

Situation: Playing a player who covers most of the court with his forehand.

Strategy: Play his backhand

Start the game by serving balls down the wall to his backhand side. This makes it impossible for him to use his forehand for the return. If he does try to use his forehand to return the serve, he will jam himself on the backhand side wall and give you a weak return or none at all.

During the game keep most of your shots down the line on your opponent's backhand side wall. Down-the-line ceiling shots to the backhand, combined with down-the-line kills and pass shots will force him into errors or make him use his weaker backhand. Keep the ball moving up and down the backhand side wall and you'll win.

Situation: Your opponent crowds you during the volley.

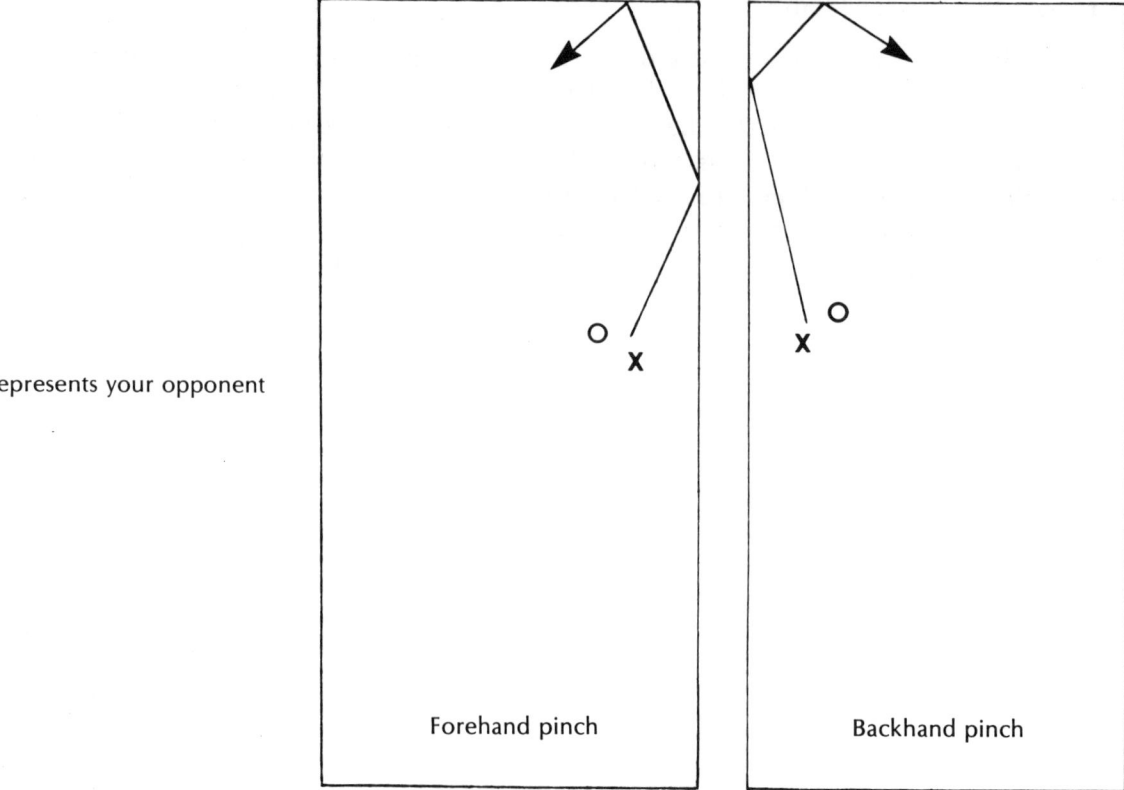

O represents your opponent

Diagrams 1 and 2. A pinch is a good alternative to an attempted cross court pass.

Strategy: Call hinders and pinch

For safety's sake, hold up your racquet before striking the ball and call a hinder when you're being crowded. This is perfectly legal and may make the point to your opponent that he is in your way and creating a dangerous situation. The referee should honor your call and warn your opponent against crowding.

For those situations where your opponent is still crowding you slightly, but not enough to cause a legal hinder, turn the tables on him. Use a low pinch to the near side wall. This will earn you a quick point at best and at least get the ball to the opposite side of the court as easily as an impaired cross court pass would have done, had he not been blocking you. The pinch is a better alternative, and worth learning and practicing. It is one of racquetball's best but least-used shots.

Situation: You crowd your opponent during the volley.

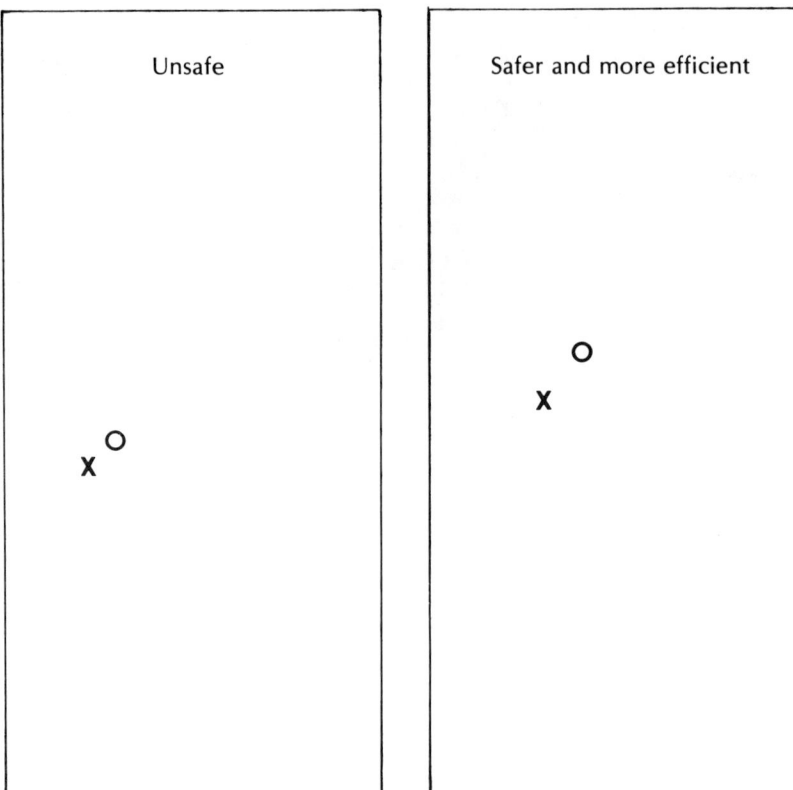

Diagrams 3 and 4. Don't crowd your opponent.

Strategy: Play safe or change your position

There are gray areas in racquetball as in any sport. Crowding your opponent as a stratagem is one of these areas. It can be dangerous, especially when you are even with your opponent on the court and you are definitely hindering him. Three possibilities present themselves. One, your opponent will hit you with his follow-through, possibly injuring you. Two, the opponent will hold up his swing in which case a hinder takes place and the point is simply replayed. The third and most detrimental to you is that the referee can call an avoidable hinder on you, awarding the point to your opponent. You lose in all three situations.

So if you are getting a lot of hinder calls, or worse, getting hit with your opponent's racquet during his follow-through, give him more room to swing by moving up more or taking a slight step to the side. This way you can safely face his side of the court and the ball in anticipation of your next shot.

Generally, playing "clean" is much more rewarding and safer than skirting the gray areas.

Situation: Your opponent watches the front wall, not the ball.

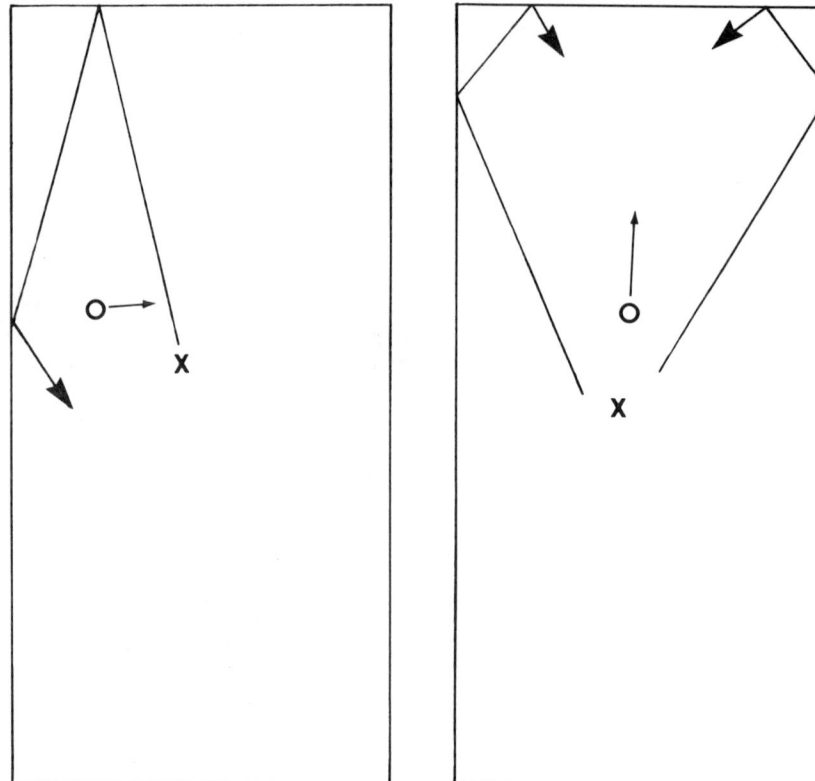

Diagram 5. (Left). Short pass for the opponent who is running to center and watching the front wall—not the ball.
Diagram 6. (Right). Low pinch from behind to force errors when your opponent watches the front wall and not the ball.

Strategy: Make him make mistakes

Since your opponent is counting on reacting to the ball as it comes off the front wall, not on anticipation as you hit the ball, you can easily trick this kind of player into making mistakes. Short pass shots and pinches easily throw this player off balance, so use them. Vary your serve from the same stance.

A short pass can easily be played off an opponent who watches the front wall and who is on one side of the court, not in the middle. As he is sliding to the middle of the court watching the front wall, zing a pass shot in the direction he's coming from. He won't be able to react in time and your point will be made. (Diagram 5.)

Pinches from behind your opponent work well to force errors. The fact that the ball is hitting the side wall first and not the front wall will throw him off balance. The angle of the ball coming off the front wall will be more difficult for him to react to and he'll stumble into front court, either missing the ball completely or retrieving a set-up for you. (Diagram 6.)

Situation: You watch the front wall, not the ball. This error usually comes from the fear of being clobbered by your opponent's racquet or the ball.

The greatest strategist of them all, Charlie Brumfield, catches an opponent staring at the wall and whips a low, right-hand corner shot in for a kill.

Strategy: With eye protection learn to watch the ball

You must break your fixation with the front wall. Get a pair of eye protectors, be brave, and start watching the ball as much as possible during the volley. Start out by watching your serves. Keep your back to your opponent and watch over the near shoulder, following the ball with your eyes. You can even hold your racquet in front of your face for added protection if your fear persists. At first you may feel a little sluggish in retrieving your opponent's shots but after a few games you'll start to react quickly to your opponent's shots and find yourself playing a better game, because you'll know where the ball is coming from and where to put it when you get your racquet on it.

Get in the habit of taking quick glances back at your opponent when you're in front of him. Try to sneak a quick backward look at the ball. You can gain more than a step if you get an early warning as to where the ball is heading. Remember handball great Paul Haber's statement, "I even watch the ball during the time-outs."

A series of quick glances at your opponent, if he's not Brumfield, will help you get a step or two lead on where the ball is going.

Situation: You've won the first serve. The coin has been tossed and you've won the right to serve first. What should your first serve be?

Strategy: Serve offensively

You are at a tremendous advantage because serving in racquetball has evolved from simply putting the ball in play to a point-making device. With today's light, whippy racquets and live balls your serving strategy should be offensive.

There are two basic offensive serves in racquetball, the drive serve and the Z serve. Both serves, when executed well, can force a weak return right away or no return for an ace. By driving the ball low and hard to your opponent's weaker side you can establish control of the match right away. You are more likely to make quick points with driving offensive serves.

The drive serve

If you have watched your opponent warm up or know which side is weaker start by attacking that weak side with a hard, driving serve. Drive serves to either side of the court can be executed successfully from three areas in the serve zone. (Diagrams 7, 8, and 9.)

Unless you have a favorite spot for drive serves to either side of the court, it is generally best to start from the center of the service zone and hit to your opponent's weaker side. This strategy gives you control of center court quicker after your serve.

The Z serve

Another variation of the aggressive, offensive first serve is to hit a low, driving Z serve to your opponent's weaker side. Z serves are generally served from an off-center position so that you are not hit by your own shot standing in center. (Diagrams 10 and 11.)

Pro Benny Koltun frequently aces Marty Hogan with his deceptive serve.

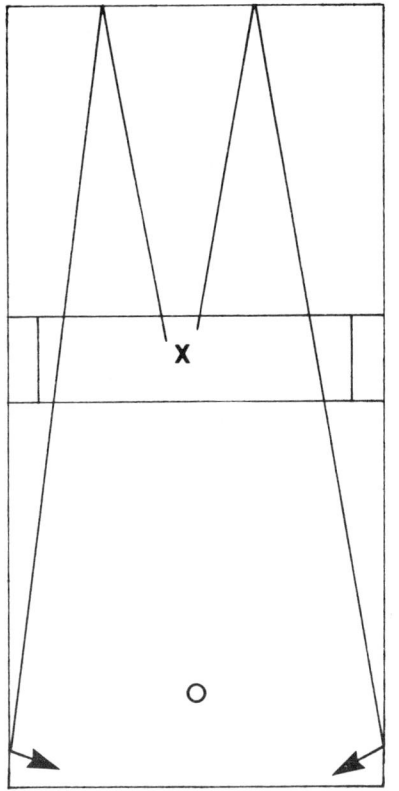 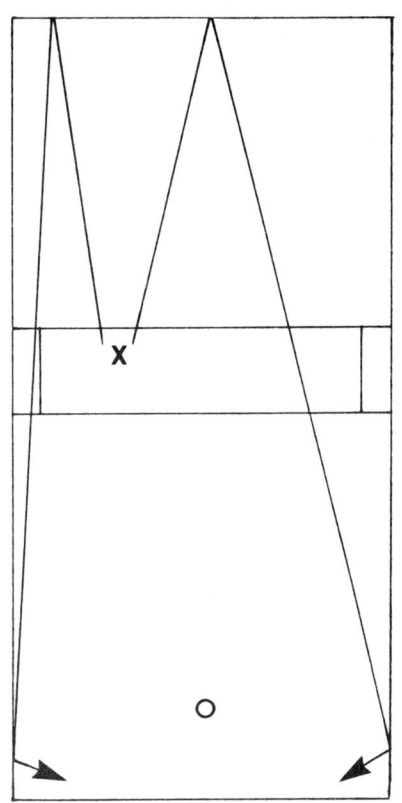 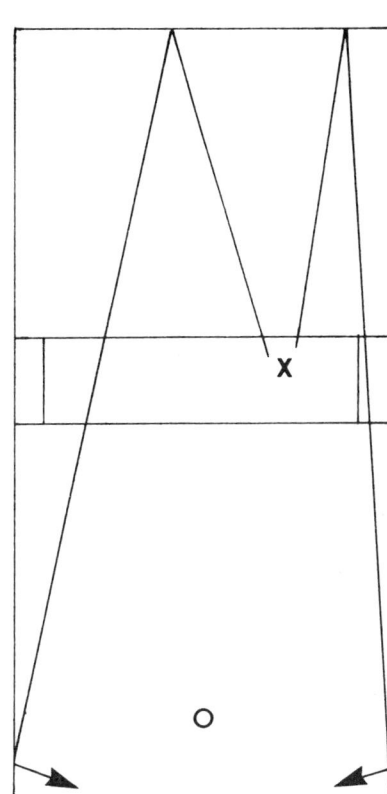

Diagrams 7, 8, and 9. The drive serve.

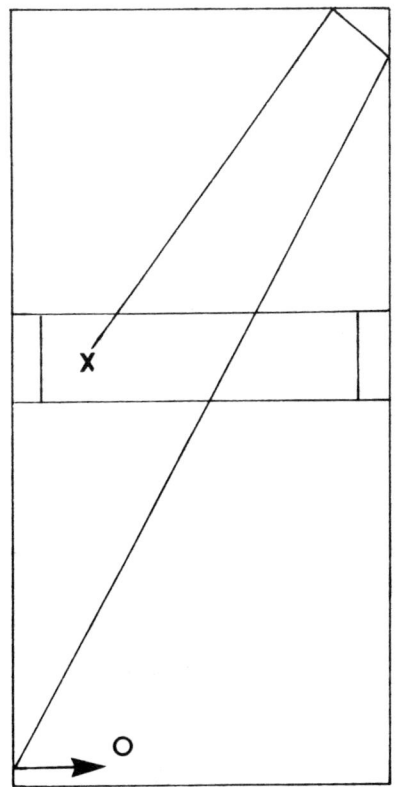 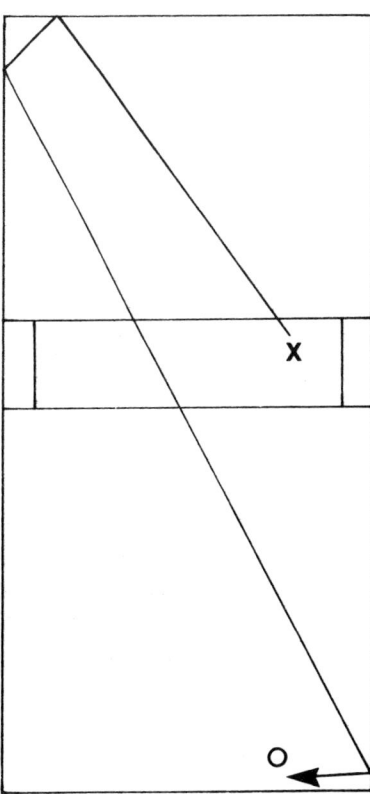

Diagram 10. (Left). The Z serve to opponent's backhand (for right-hand receivers).

Diagram 11. (Right). the Z serve to opponent's forehand.

Situation: You are receiving the first serve, a drive or a Z serve.

Strategy: Use good receiving position and capitalize on errors

Position yourself in the middle of deep court, a little more than an arm's and racquet's length from the back wall. Focus your attention on the ball as your opponent sets up to hit it.

Execution: To return drive serves:

1. Move up. It may throw your opponent off by making him try too hard to serve the ball past you.
2. As the ball comes over the short line, turn and get ready to hit it, but do not move over and crowd the ball.
3. Determine which wall the ball will strike first.

> a. If the ball strikes the side wall and pops up for set-up, kill it. A corner pinch will work best in this situation. (Diagram 12.) The corner pinch works best because your opponent is backing out of the service zone toward center court. The pinch gives him no chance of recovering the ball.
> b. If the ball strikes the side wall first but is not a set-up, return a ceiling shot down the line near the left or right wall. To try and do more with an effective drive serve will probably result in your giving your opponent a set-up. (Diagram 13.)
> c. If your opponent's serve is coming around the corner and off the back wall you have two good options, either of which should win you an immediate side-out if executed well. You can kill the ball or pass the ball. (Diagrams 14 and 15.)
> d. If the ball goes into the back wall first and pops out for a set-up you have three good options. You can kill it straight-in. (Diagram 16.) You can hit the ball into

Safe receiver positioning—it's best to stay deep until you know the nature of your opponent's serve.

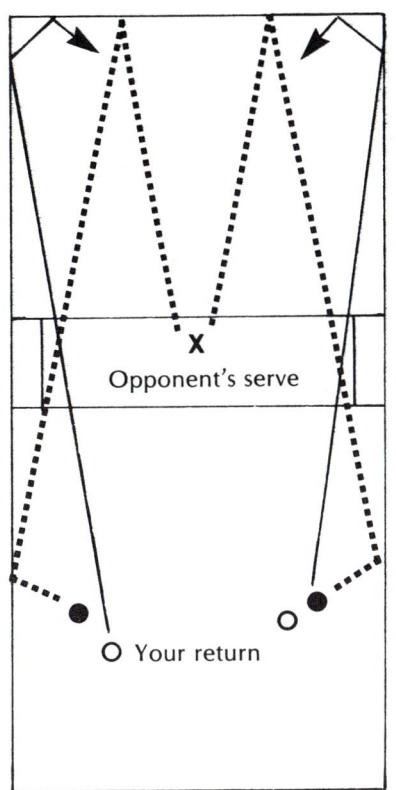

Diagram 12. The corner pinch works best because your opponent is backing out of the service zone toward center court. The pinch gives him no chance of recovering the ball.

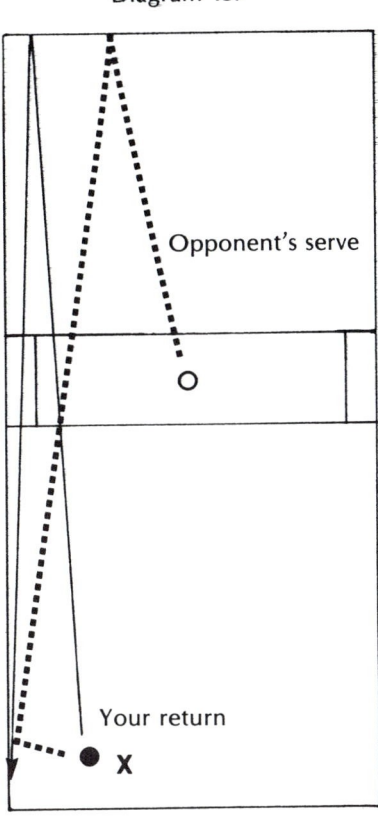

Diagram 13.

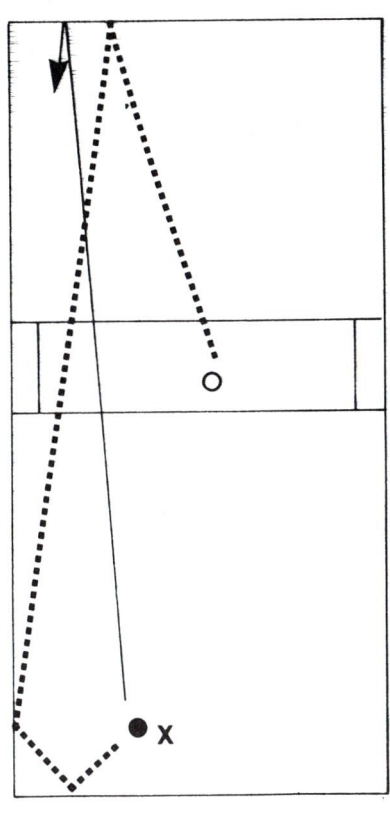

Diagram 14. Straight kill. Option 1.

(Far left). If your opponent is drive serving accurately, move up, the move will throw your foe's serve off, and if he is a hot-head, your seemingly ⎯⎯ move will cause him to tighten up and lose c⎯

(Near left). If the ball pops out of the ⎯

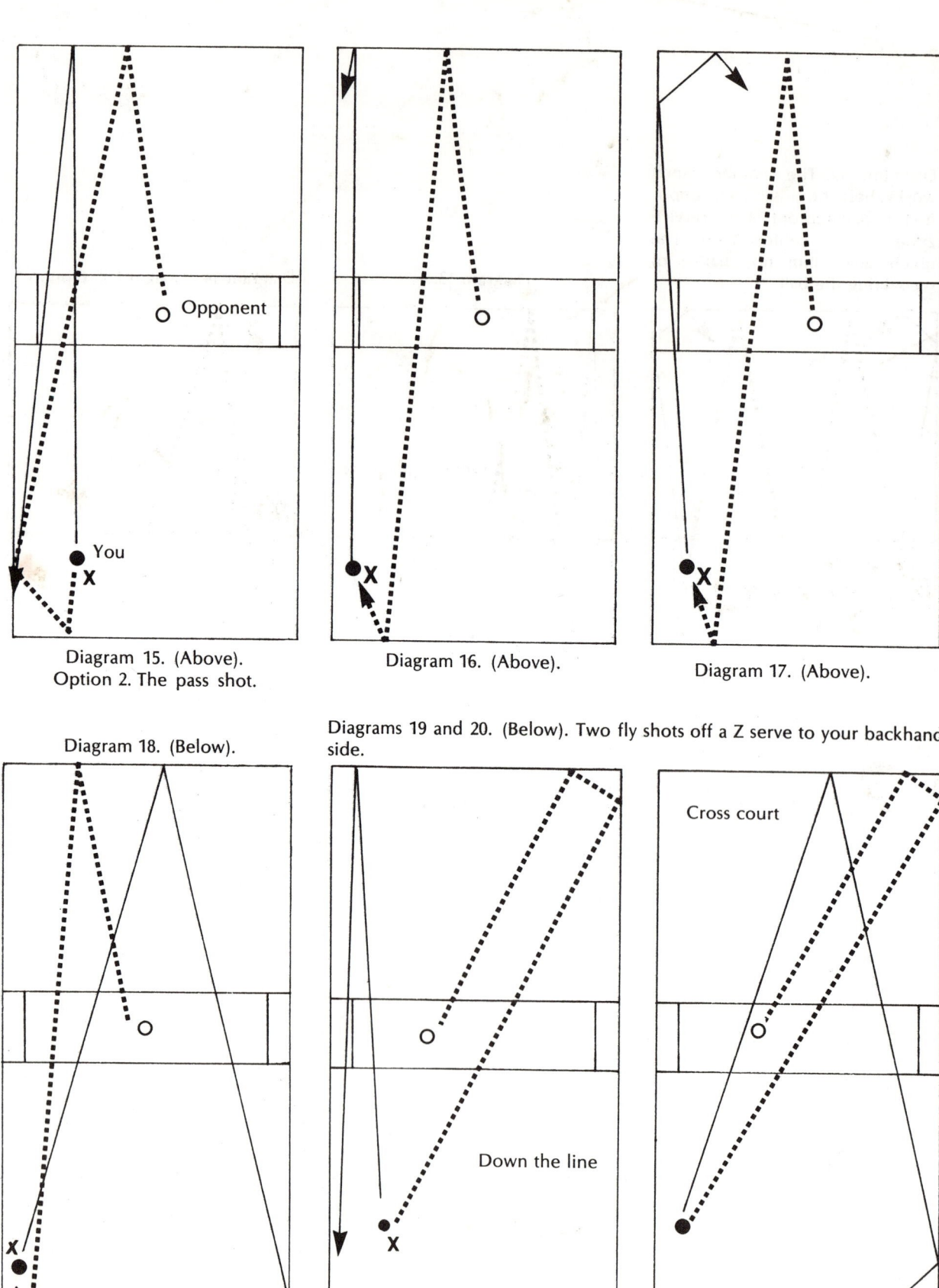

Diagram 15. (Above). Option 2. The pass shot.

Diagram 16. (Above).

Diagram 17. (Above).

Diagram 18. (Below).

Diagrams 19 and 20. (Below). Two fly shots off a Z serve to your backhand side.

Down the line

Cross court

If you're returning a drive serve off the back wall, as Don Pydo does here, try to kill in the left corner, or pass to your opponent with a hard-hit shot.

the left "pinch" corner—left wall-front wall. (Diagram 17.)

If your opponent starts to drift back on the backhand side you can hit a cross court pass shot for a winner. (Diagram 18.)

Execution: To return the Z serve:

Fly shoot the ball—that is, hit it before it bounces on the floor—before it gets to the side wall and causes you problems. When you cut the ball off on a fly, pass it around your opponent either down the line or cross court. There is a surprise element working for you when you hit a fly shot. (Diagrams 19 and 20.)

If you can hit a fly shot off the first attempt your opponent makes at a Z serve you can intimidate him away from serving it again, especially if your return is an effective one.

Execution: Other returns for the Z serve:

If the ball hits the side wall and comes up short, enabling you to wait and execute a sidearm stroke, try to pass your opponent or kill the ball.

If the ball jams you coming off the side wall at chest level, return a ceiling shot, if you can get set for one.

If the ball comes around off the back wall, try to kill it.

Situation: Playing a player who covers most of the court with a backhand.

Strategy: Play his forehand

Don't be afraid to play his forehand. You may find it nonexistent. Surprise drive serves to the forehand may catch him off guard and force him to make errors. Use cross-court passes to his deep forehand corner of the court. This will be the only place he cannot back up to take a backhand shot.

Situation: You've given your opponent a set-up off the back wall.

Strategy: Watch your opponent and anticipate his shot

Watch your opponent as he sets up to shoot the ball. You may be able to detect where he will hit the ball before he does. Move to center and, if possible without causing a hinder, move slightly to the side of the court your opponent is on as he shoots. This maneuver will take away his cross-court pass and force him to shoot the ball to your side of the court. You at least have a chance of recovering the ball if it comes up high.

Try to determine the shot he is likely to try. You may even try to force that shot by standing in the position that will make him shoot it, then as his eyes drop to the ball to hit it change your position to the one that will cover his shot.

Another trick—if you know your opponent can't kill the ball off the back wall you may deliberately stay back a little and let him try. You may get a skip ball or a ball left up in center court for you to run forward and kill.

Properly anticipating your opponent's off-the-back-wall shot helps you move efficiently to your next shot as sharp-eyed lawyer Tony Buckun does against Don Pydo.

Situation: Your opponent has given you a set-up off the back wall.

Strategy: Shoot the ball

1. The back wall set-up is as favorable to most good players as getting a set-up in center court. In fact, it is the "second center court" to all pros. First, kill the ball if you can (as National Champion Shannon Wright is doing against co-author Jean Sauser in the photo). Tilling should be your first priority as you get better. Shoot to the near corner as you set up to take the ball off the back wall. (See Diagrams 21 and 22.)

2. Use the straight kill to the open side of the court if your opponent has hit the ball up the middle of the court, forcing him out of center. (Diagrams 23 and 24.)

3. Pass for points only if your opponent gets overanxious and moves too far forward to cover your kill. (Diagrams 25 and 26.)

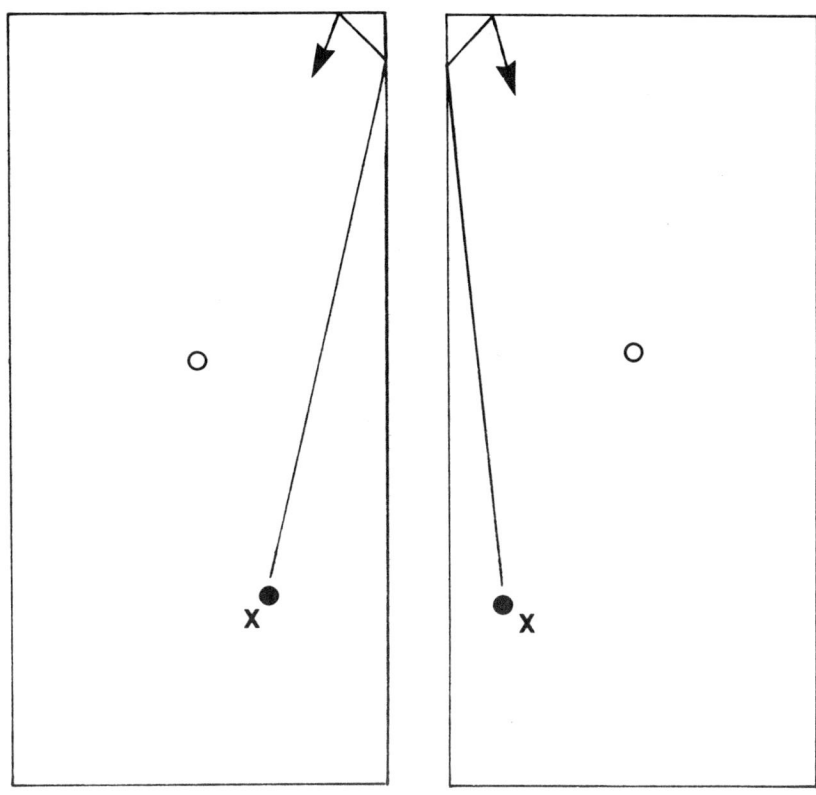

Diagram 21. Diagram 22.

Diagrams 23 and 24. Straight kill to the open side.

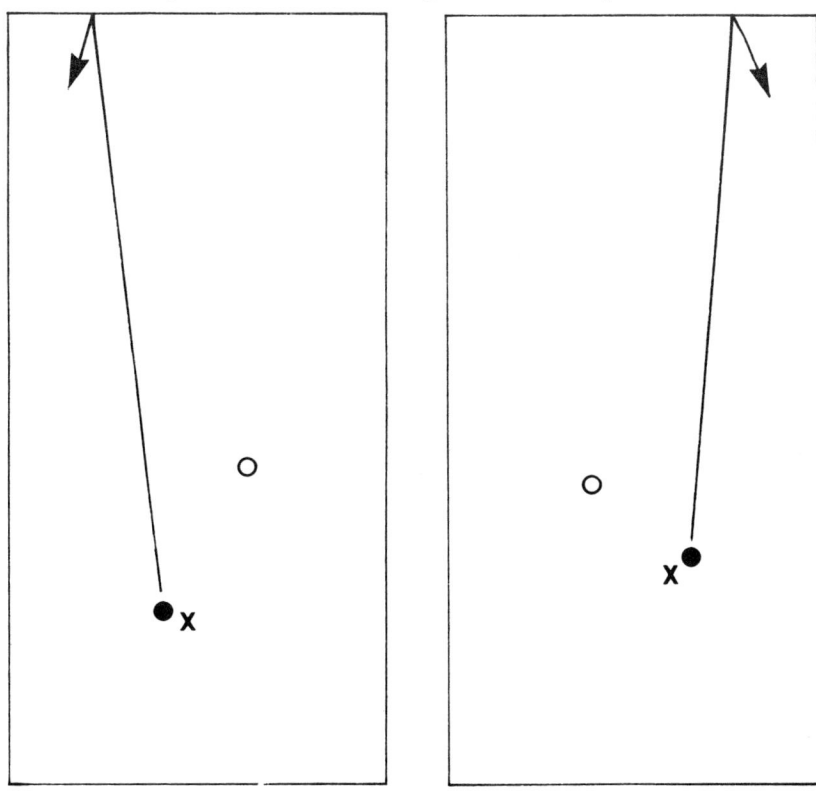

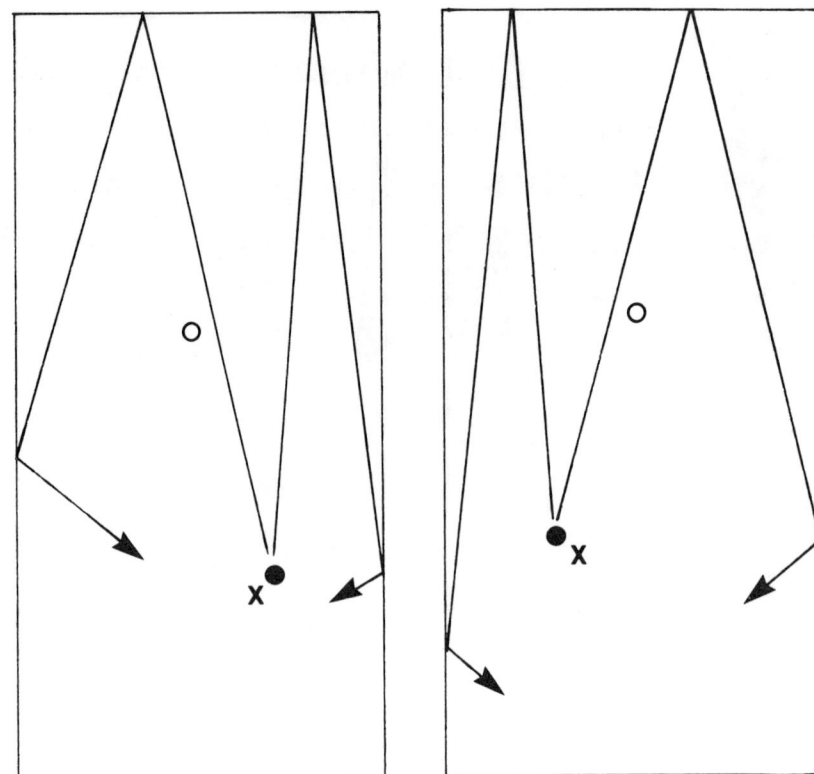

Diagrams 25 and 26. Pass for points.

Situation: You've given your opponent a front wall/back wall set-up shot—that is, you've hit the ball to the front wall hard enough so that it comes off the back wall for an easy shot by your foe.

Strategy: Anticipate from center court

Don't give up. Hurry to center court position and focus your complete attention on the ball. You'll be able to anticipate the next shot by watching your opponent's racquet swing. The arc of the swing telegraphs the shot that will result. So stay on your toes and get ready to recover the second you see the direction the ball is going.

Situation: Your opponent gives you a front wall/back wall set-up. You are now running toward the front wall space with the ball. As you are waiting for the ball to drop, you find that when you do hit the ball you will be too far forward in front court.

Strategy: Kill, pinch, or pass

In this situation you have three shots to choose from. You can hit the ball straight in for a kill, pinch to the near corner, or pass it across to the opposite side of the court for a wide angle low pass. (You can also bobble—but let's not!)

1. Straight kill: This works best on either side of the court if your opponent comes to center court while you are hitting the ball. If you kill the ball successfully, the point is yours. If you hit the ball too high for a good kill, it may still turn into a good down-the-line pass that will possibly win you the point, or at least give you time to get back to center court while your opponent scurries after your shot. (Diagrams 27 and 28.)

2. Pinch: This works if you are not too close to the front wall when contacting the ball, and if your opponent is on the same side of the court you are. (Diagrams 29 and 30.)

3. Wide angle low pass: This shot works if your opponent makes the mistake of coming up just in front of center court. Your shot should strike the front wall low and hard, angling away and, with luck, catching a "crack" (where the floor meets the wall) either directly across from where your opponent is standing or slightly behind him for the winner. (Diagrams 31 and 32.)

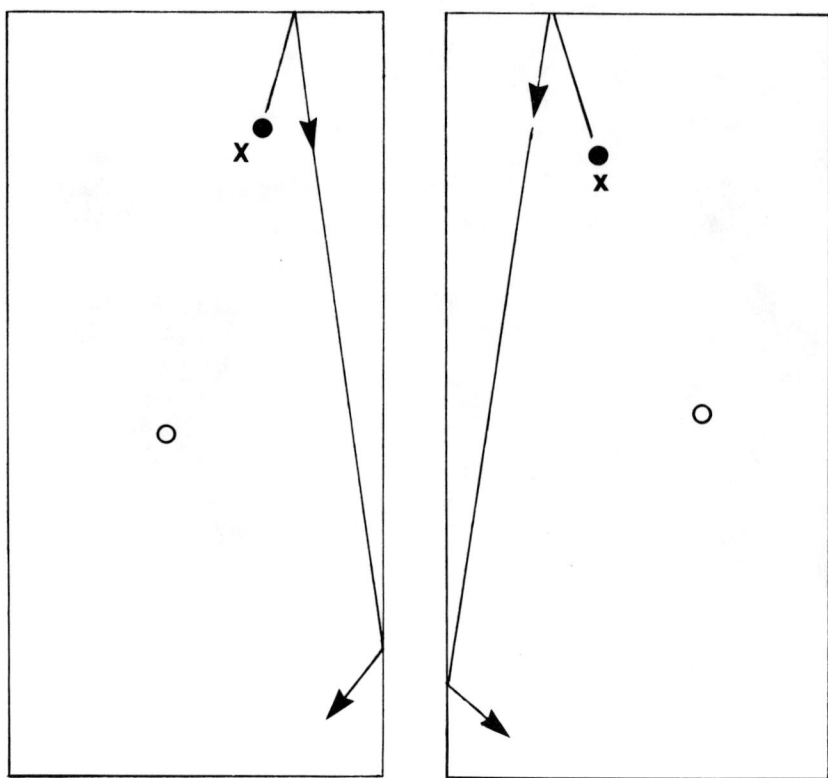
Diagrams 27 and 28. Straight kill for the front wall/back wall set-up.

Diagrams 29 and 30. Pinch.
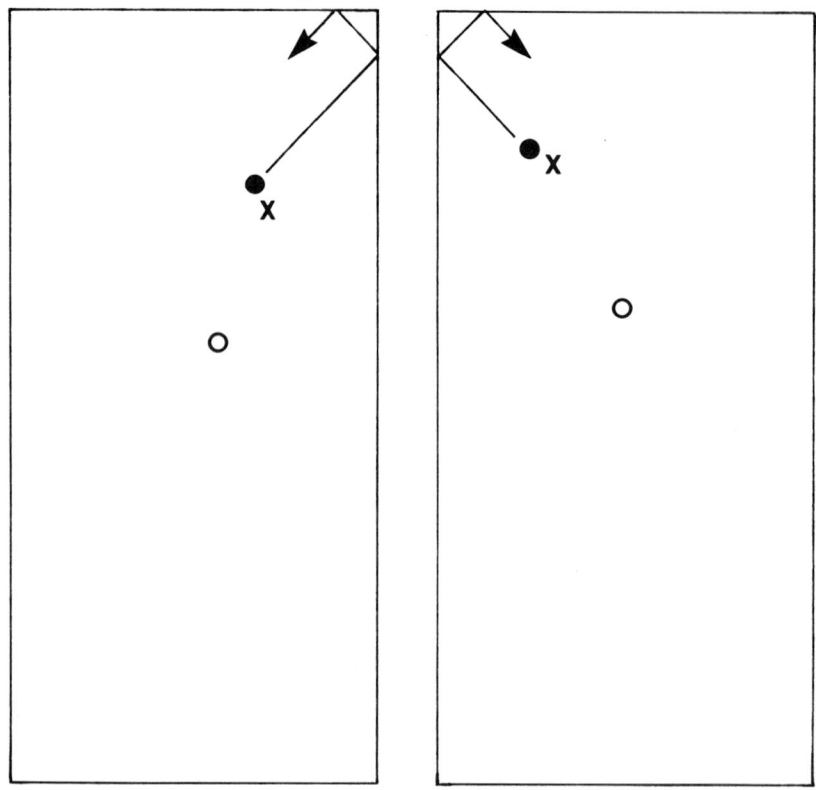

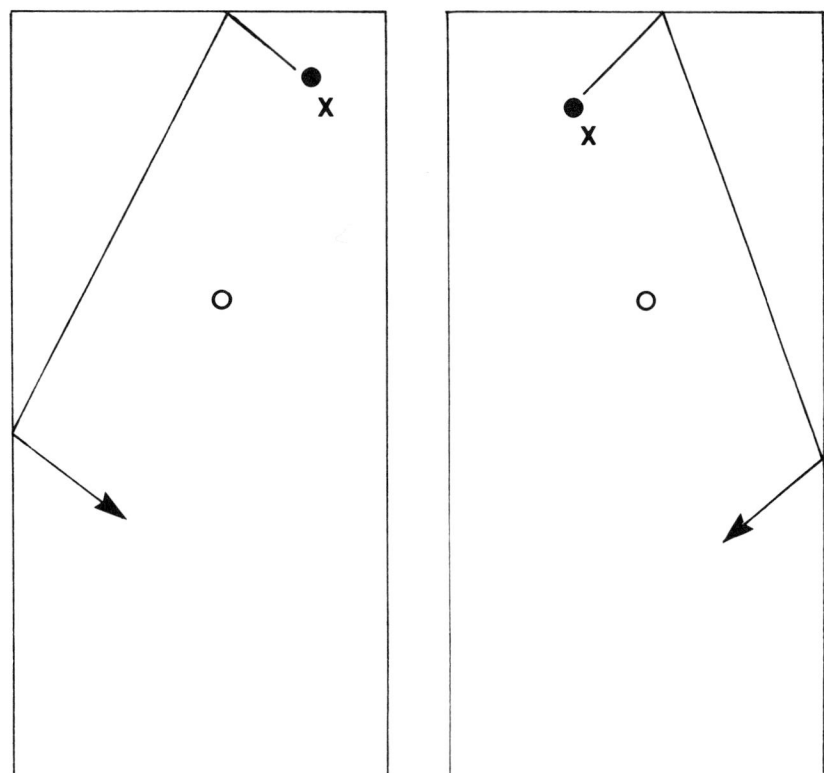
Diagrams 31 and 32. Wide angle low pass.

Situation: You are forced to hit the ball into the back wall first.

Strategy: Reverse ceiling ball

If at all possible, hit under the ball, so it will rebound high on its way to the front wall, hopefully catching the ceiling and coming back as a ceiling shot. If you can't do this, try to make an angle that will cause the ball to come off the front wall close enough to a side wall so that your opponent cannot fly-kill it. (Diagram 33.) Turn and get back to center court or as close to center court as possible without hindering your opponent.

Diagram 33. Desperation-into-the-back-wall shot. Keep the ball out of center.

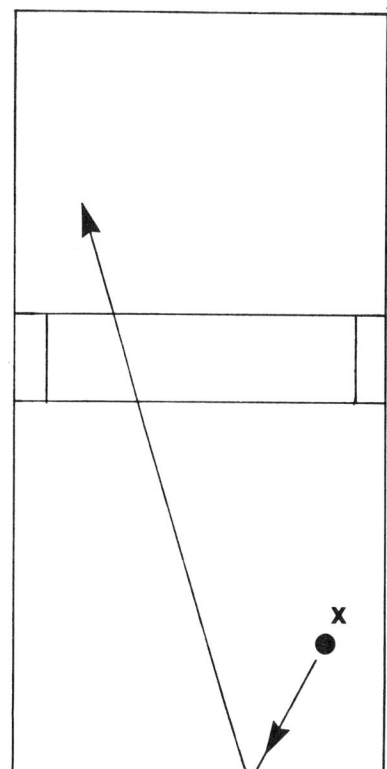

Situation: Your opponent has slammed the ball into the back wall, on a desperation play. The ball has carried to the front wall and is now coming down. He is out of position or unbalanced.

Strategy: Fly kill

Fly kill. (Return the ball before it bounces on the floor.) This is the first priority. Anytime you have your opponent running away from center court with his back to you and the ball comes off the front wall slow and on the fly, set up and fly-kill it, to the same side of the court you're facing. Surprise and power are on your side here. To wait for this ball to bounce and turn into a set-up in deep court allows your opponent time to get back into center court position, his best position for recovering anything you do. Fly killing enables you to cut his reaction time in half and even if your shot isn't perfect, it will probably still make the point, because he is too far out of position and off balance to recover even an inaccurate shot.

Situation: Receiving during the first ten points of the game.

Strategy: Use effective shot selection

As in serving, you want to vary your returns in order to find out which ones are most effective in winning you a side-out.

If you are playing an out-of-shape player who has good center court strategy, your serve returns should probably be wide-angle, cross-court pass shots, forcing him to run as far as possible for the ball.

If you are playing an opponent who drifts back too far after completing his serve, you should try to kill the ball he served you, if possible.

Situation: Serving when both scores are under ten points in the first half of the game. The match has begun and you are in the first stages of the game. What should your serving combinations be?

Strategy: Vary your serves

In addition to striving for accuracy when serving, it is important to establish an effective pace and to vary your serves.

The rules of racquetball state that you have ten seconds to put the ball in play. Take your time and make a mental picture of the serve you are about to hit. Then drop the ball and serve. Your chances of accuracy will increase with visualization.

It is important to serve a variety of serves from a variety of locations in the service zone for two reasons. First, you want to find out which gives your opponent the most trouble. Use the first points of the game to experiment a little and find out. Second, if you vary the

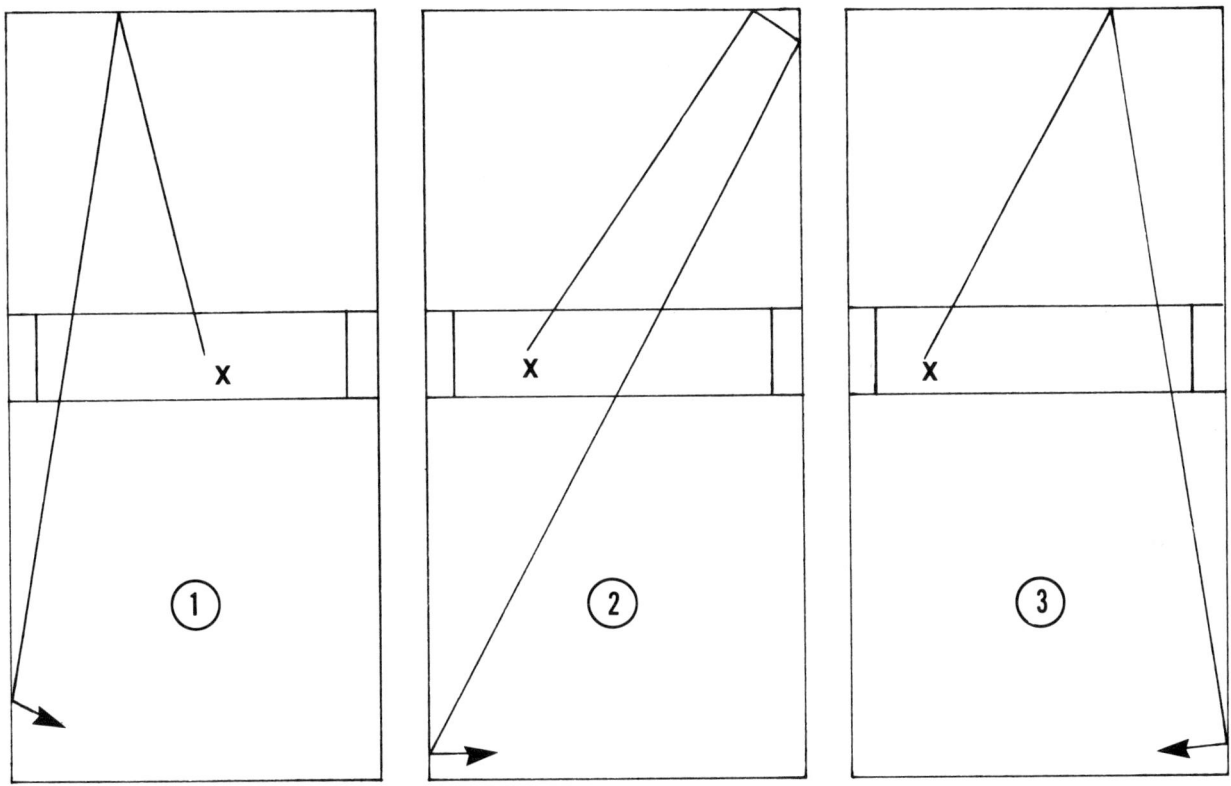

Diagrams 34, 35, and 36. Serve Combination A.

(Far left). Serving from the far left, you can drive serve, Z serve, lob serve, or garbage serve to either side. All of your options are open.

(Center left). Serving from the center is the safest because you can easily get to center court to cover your opponent's return. From here you can drive, lob, or garbage serve to either side of the court. Serves can be done from center but are a little more difficult.

(Near left). Serving from the far right: All serves are possible from this location. Good for serving lefthanders.

41

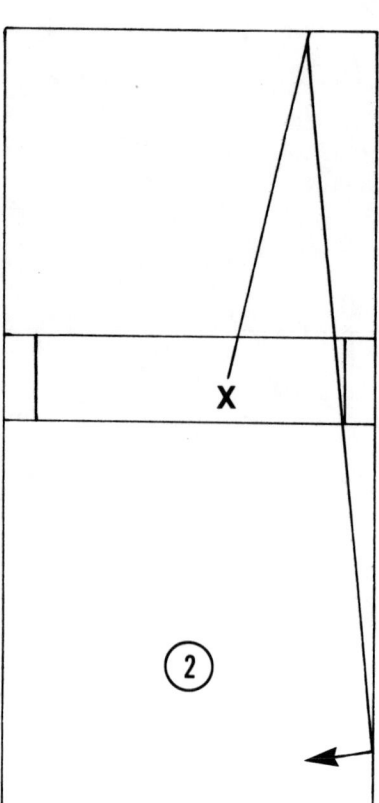

Diagrams 37 and 38. (Left). Serve Combination B.

Diagrams 39, 40, and 41. (Below). Serve Combination C.

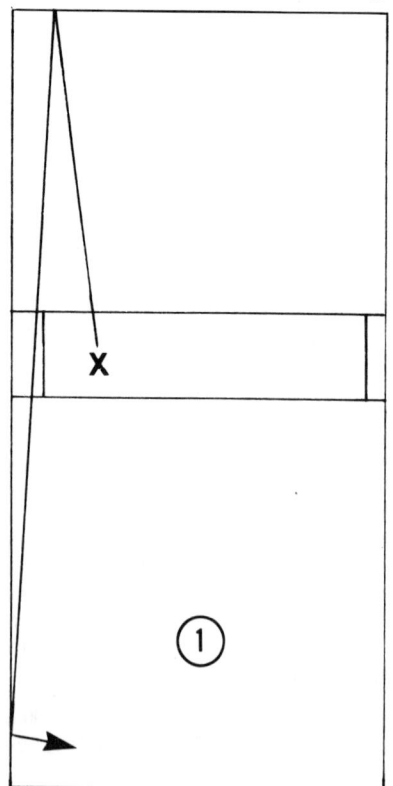
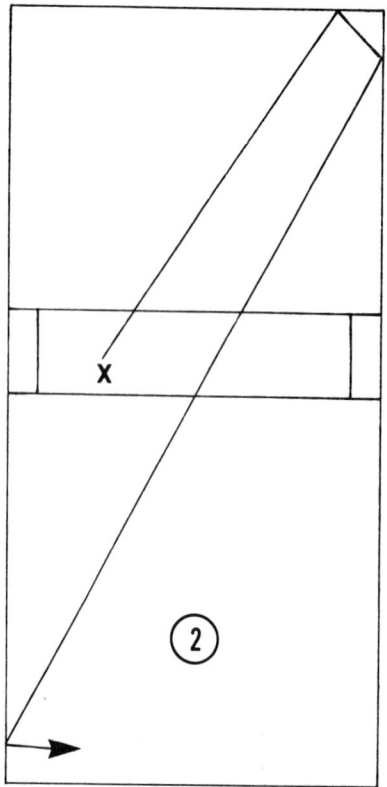
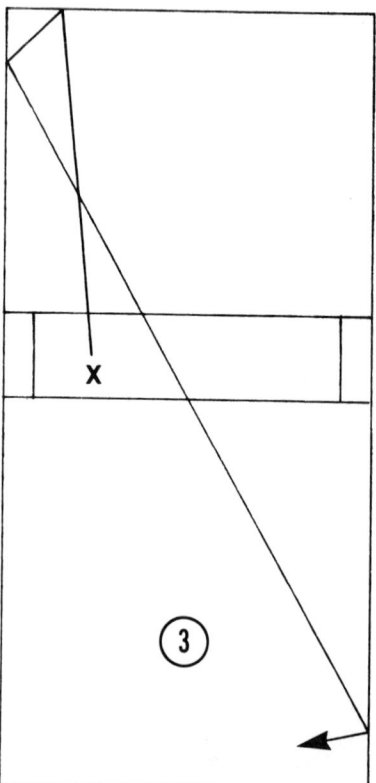

types of serves you use and the places in the service zone you stand when you serve, you can trick your opponent into expecting one kind of serve, but receiving another, putting him off balance physically as well as mentally. See combinations A, B, and C.

To vary your serve combinations develop the ability to serve every serve from the right of center of the service zone, the left of center, and in the center of the service zone. Here are some suggested serve combinations that can get you on your way to beating your opponent within the first half of the game.

Suggested serve combination A
1. Serve a few drive serves from the center to your opponent's backhand.
2. Then serve some low, hard Z serves from off center to your opponent's backhand.
3. Once you see that your opponent is leaning to the backhand side in anticipation of a Z or drive to the backhand, drive a low, fast, wide-angle drive serve to his forehand for the ace.

Suggested serve combination B
1. From right of center, serve some drive serves to your opponent's backhand.
2. Then from the same position, serve a fast down-the-line drive to the forehand side of the court.

Suggested serve combination C
1. Drive some narrow-angle drive serves to your opponent's backhand.
2. Drive some low, hard Z serves, again to his backhand.
3. Serve a reverse Z serve to your opponent's forehand.

Other combinations in serving might include changing the speed of the ball. You can, for example, serve a series of medium-speed garbage serves and then quickly hit a low, hard drive. Or reverse it: hit a series of drives to either side of the court and then change up with a slow tempting lob serve. Change in speed on the ball can surprise your opponent, and he'll tend to overreact to the ball, giving you a set-up, or better yet, no return.

Situation: You have only one serve attempt left.

In an attempt to serve an ace with the first ball, you have hit short or long. This is a situation that can happen frequently in a racquetball match. You now have one chance left to put the ball in play. Which serve should you use?

Strategy: Use a defensive serve

Don't try for an ace. That's doubling the pressure on yourself. Use your second serve for intelligent ball placement, geared to receiving a defensive return. There are two defensive serves in racquetball, the half-lob, or garbage serve, and the lob serve.

The lob serve:

The idea is to hit the ball high on the front wall and as lightly as possible to prevent a back wall set-up. Contact the ball at waist level or above waist level. Use a "helping" motion instead of a hitting motion. The ball should travel three-quarters of the way up on the front wall first, then rebound along the side wall, bouncing over your opponent's head into the deep corner of the court. If your serve is a good one all your opponent can do is return a ceiling shot.

Both lob and garbage serves can be served from anywhere in the service zone, like drive serves. If you have a special "touch" for serving the ball in one particular spot make sure you serve from there. If you are not sure where you should stand, serve from the center of the service zone to allow yourself maximum center court coverage of your opponent's return. (Diagrams 44, 45, and 46.)

The garbage serve:

This is the best second serve to use because the ball is easily controlled. Serve from the

Diagram 42. (Below). Lob serve—side view.

Diagram 43. (Right). Lob serve—basic angle.

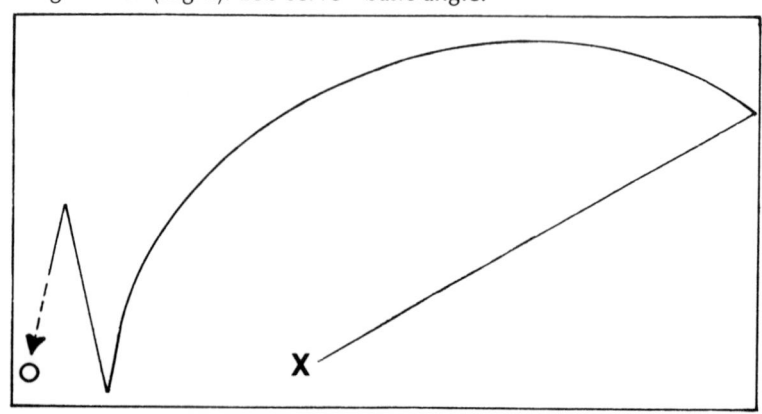
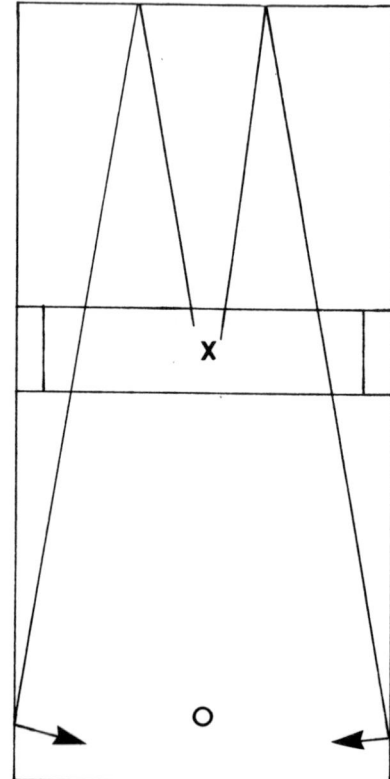

Slowing up and serving a more defensive serve on the second serve after committing a fault is strongly advised.

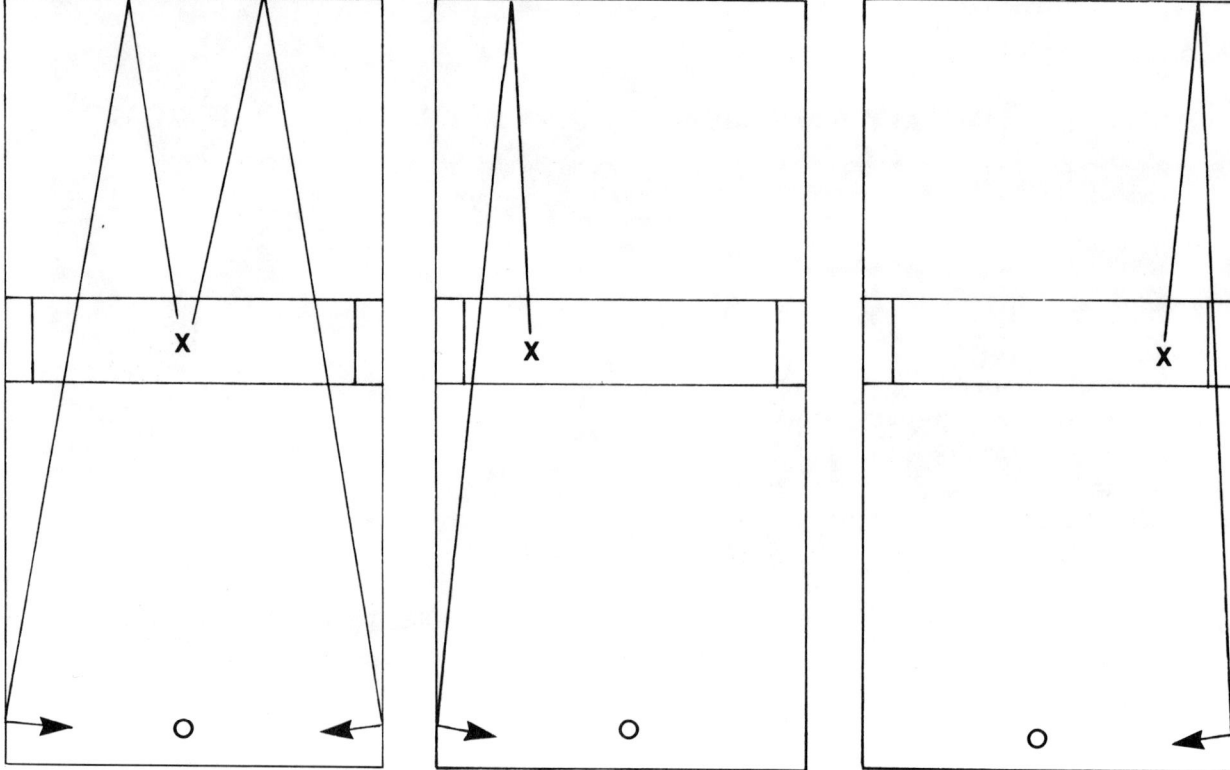

Diagrams 44-46. Variations of lob and garbage serves.

center of your service zone so that you can effectively cover your opponent's return. Use a forehand stroke and contact the ball at waist level. The ball should then bounce past the short line—not as high as a lob—and rebound along the side wall into the deep corner of the court. Your opponent will be forced to contact the ball also at waist level or slightly above. If he is smart he won't try to do anything more with this serve than return a defensive ceiling shot. If he does try to shoot the ball, he may skip it or leave it up for you to put away easily in center court. (Diagrams 47 and 48.)

Diagrams 47 and 48. It's safe to serve the garbage serve from center so you can cover your opponent's return. Below left is side view.

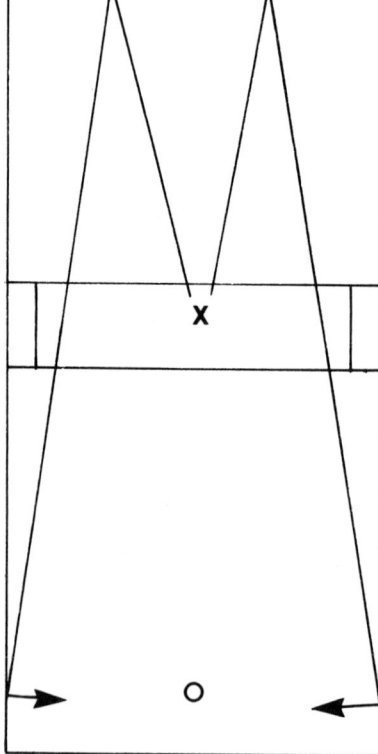

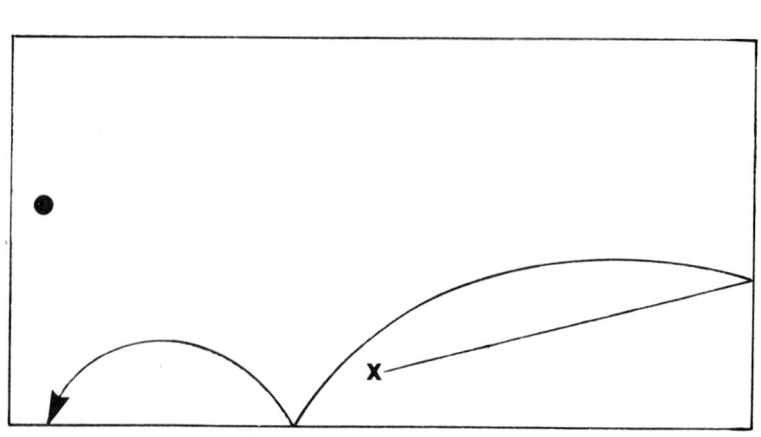

Situation: You are serving and are winning the game.

Strategy: Play aggressively

1. Play as aggressively as you can, using ace hard serves and hard shots.

2. Use the serve or serving combination that is winning you points until it fails to keep doing so. If you've found one serve your opponent is not capable of returning effectively, service this relentlessly through to point 21.

3. Don't experiment. Stay with what is working.

National champion, Leach's Marty Hogan concentrates on serving.

Situation: One serve to come. You're receiving and your opponent serves you a garbage or lob serve.

Strategy: Use a ceiling return

(Returning the garbage serve.) If it's an effective garbage serve, the best return is a ceiling ball. To try and kill could result in a skip ball or a set-up to the server. You can use a down-the-line ceiling ball or a cross-court ceiling ball to effectively remove your opponent from center court.

Strategy: Play aggressively

(Returning the lob serve.) If it's accurate, and too close to the side wall for you to pick off on the fly, then use a ceiling return. If it is far enough away from the side wall for you to get your racquet on it, try to kill the ball or drive it cross court past your opponent on the fly.

Returning an effective garbage or lob serve requires a defensive ceiling ball return as illustrated here by pros Kathy Williams and Jane Marriott.

The ceiling ball return off a defensive serve.

If the serve-ball is not glued to the side wall, cut if off on the fly to kill or pass.

Fly kill off the defensive serve.

Situation: You are receiving and your opponent is ahead.

It's that terrible situation where your opponent can do nothing wrong; all his serves are aces or near aces. He's putting away every return for a point. You're staring at defeat.

Strategy: Use your time-outs to change the pace

1. Call a time-out. This may cool down your opponent.

2. If the time-out works and he gives you a less effective serve, attack it and try for a kill shot, a perfect pass, or other winner—your best effort.

3. If your foe's serves are still effective, slow up the play by driving the ball to the ceiling. The ceiling ball will at least move him out of center court and give you a chance to move him around, possibly forcing him into an error or two.

Marty Hogan calls a time-out.

Situation: The score is close and you've just won the volley for your twentieth point. With a sigh of relief you step into the service zone.

Strategy: Wait, concentrate, then serve

The twenty-first point is the most important point in racquetball. The serve you choose should be the most accurate one you've hit in the game so far. Use the following steps to deliver a winning serve.

1. Take your time: You'll want to make the most of the ten seconds you have to serve the ball. Not only does this put pressure on your opponent and force him to think about the fact that you're about to win, but you'll need the time to choose the best serve possible.

2. Pick the serve that has won you the most points during the match. With this type of shot you'll increase your chances for an ace.

3. Concentrate: Picture the serve in your mind in its most perfect form. Once you can clearly see it, serve the ball.

Situation: Your opponent is serving the game point.

Strategy: Call time-out and react to the serve, not the score

Call a time-out if:

1. Your opponent has rolled up a series of points that have put him up to that twentieth point. This can stop his momentum substantially enough to affect his serve.

2. You are slightly tired from the previous volley. Give yourself a chance to rest and prepare to receive the serve.

Other things to remember: No matter what the score, the important thing to do is react to the serve and not the score. You must choose the correct return. There is nothing you can do to change the score except choose a good return to earn a side-out.

Situation: You correctly anticipate and are able to intercept your opponent's cross-court pass to your forehand side.

Strategy: Pinch or pass down the line

The two major shots to use are a pinch to the forehand corner and a down-the-line shot to the forehand side. Above all, do not blast the ball cross-court to the backhand side he is coming from. Pinch or pass. (Diagrams 49 and 50.)

Diagram 49. (Below, left). Pinch if your opponent is in deep court.

Diagram 50. (Below, right). Pass if your opponent is close to center court or coming up quickly.

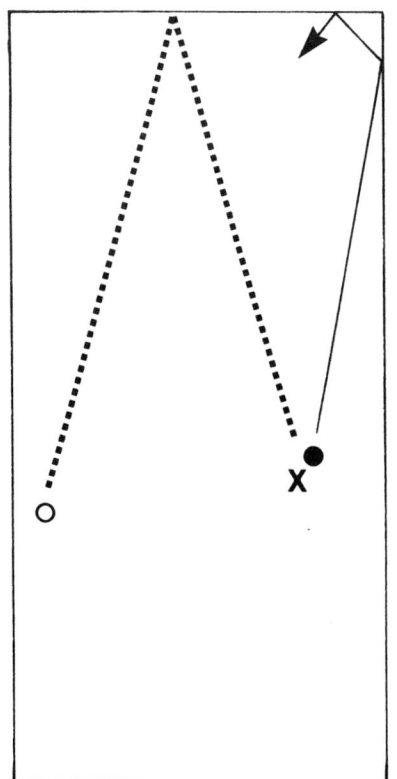
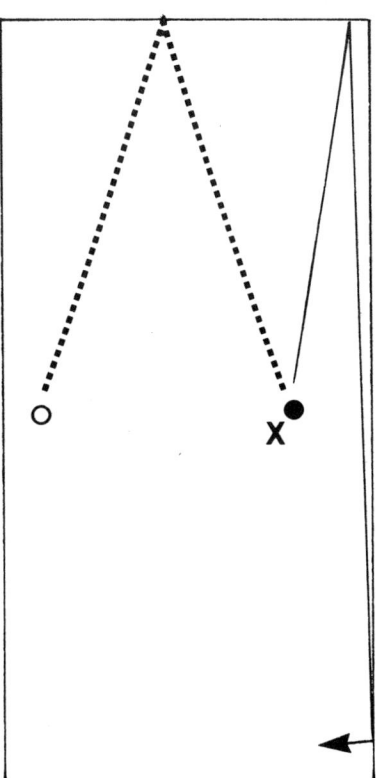

Situation: Your opponent has intercepted your cross-court pass to his forehand and is about to shoot the ball.

Strategy: Anticipate from center court

Come to center court facing his side of the court but avoid leaning in his direction. (You'll never be able to recover a pinch shot if you do.) You can now recover the pinch or cut off his attempt at a down-the-line shot. Stay well balanced on the balls of your feet for a fast change of position.

Situation: From behind you, your opponent shoots a down-the-line shot to your backhand. You've anticipated the shot and are moving across the court to cut if off before it gets by you.

Strategy: Pinch

Pinch the ball into the backhand corner by hitting the ball into the backhand side wall. (Diagram 51.)

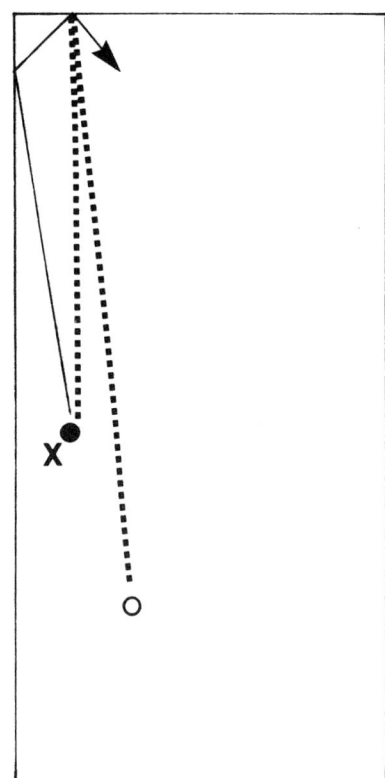

Diagram 51. Cutting off your opponent's down-the-line shot. Pinch for the quick point.

Situation: Your opponent has reached your down-the-line shot and is about to cut it off.

Strategy: Stay in his blind spot

Come forward to center court position but remain in his blind spot, behind him. Don't let him see you. Not knowing where you are makes his shot selection harder. If he should pinch the ball you can run to the center to try and retrieve it. If he tries to pass, you can probably recover his shot because of the lead time you will have to anticipate it. (Diagram 52.)

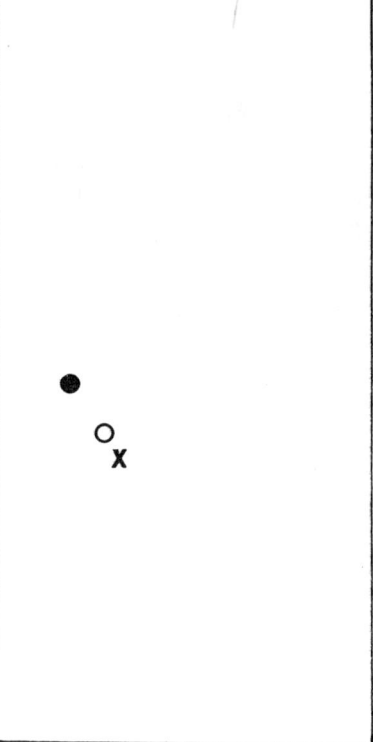

Diagram 52. Staying in your opponent's blind spot makes shot selection harder for him.

Situation: Your opponent is chasing your pass shot around the backhand corner with his forehand and returns it strongly, trying to pinch it into your forehand corner or pass you.

Strategy: Anticipate to the forehand side of the court

Turn with him and position. If necessary, to prevent being hit, position yourself slightly to the left of center court, ready to move toward the ball.

Situation: You've chased your opponent's cross-court pass around your backhand corner with your forehand and are in trouble and off balance.

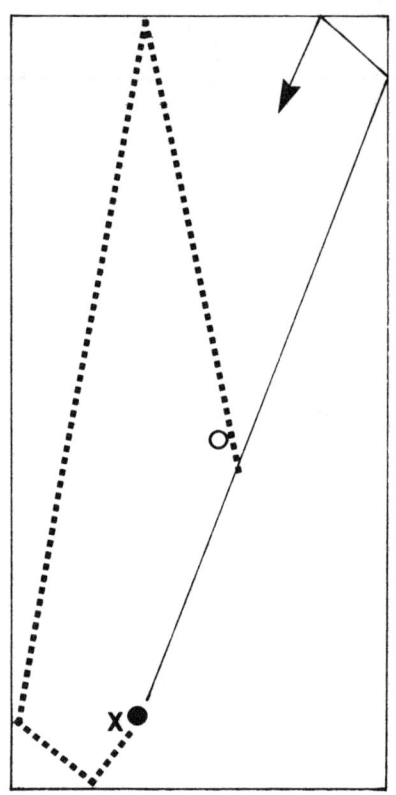
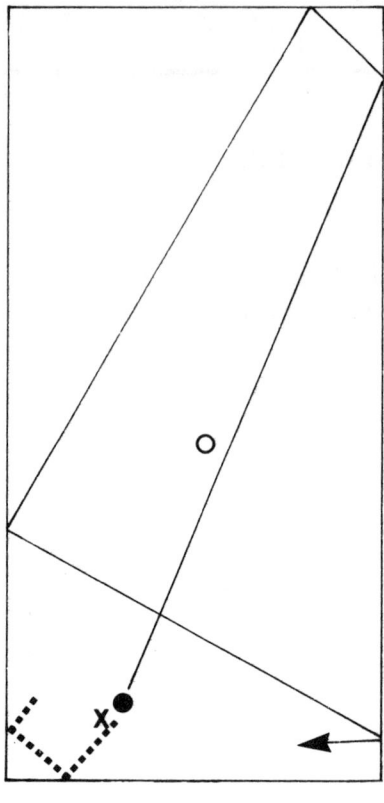

Diagram 53. (Far left). Pinch.

Diagram 54. (Left). Around-the-wall ball.

Strategy: Hit in the direction of the ball

No matter where your opponent positions himself, if you are off balance you have one good alternative, go with the direction of the ball. Hit the ball across the court to the forehand front corner. The poorer alternative is to hit an around-the-wall ball. These are the two easiest shots to hit from this off-balance position. (Diagrams 53 and 54.)

Situation: Your opponent's intended right corner kill has come up high enough for you to retrieve the ball in front court.

Strategy: Re-kill down the line

Re-kill down the left line immediately, straight into the front wall. (Diagram 55.)

Diagram 55.

Situation: Your attempted corner kill has come up too high. Your opponent is racing toward the ball to recover it.

Strategy: Stay in the play

Stay up front. Force your opponent to try and pass you. The angle of your shot will be a difficult one to contend with and if he fails to re-kill the ball, he'll leave it up high enough for you to chase down. If you drift back expecting a pass you'll never be able to come forward in time to recover a kill or attempted kill that lands in front court again.

Situation: You have a set-up in center court. Both you and your opponent are in center court.

Strategy: Straight kill or down-the-line pass

Simply turn your back to your opponent and shoot the ball into the front wall for a straight kill or a down-the-line winner. Legally you can screw the ball this way as the rules state you have the right of way in the court when you are hitting the ball. Either shot will make the point. If the situation repeats itself as it often does, you can alternate the two shots to confuse your opponent and keep him off balance.

Situation: You have given your opponent a set-up and you are both in center court.

Strategy: Stay in front court

Stay forward and turn slightly toward the side of the court the ball is on. You can now anticipate what your opponent will do with the ball. If he misses his shot or returns weakly you can easily run over and recover the ball. Do not drop back out of center expecting a pass shot. If you drop back your opponent can easily kill the ball or switch his shot to a corner pinch. By staying up you put pressure on him to shoot a pinpoint kill or a perfect pass—two unlikely events in beginners play.

Situation: Your opponent has, during a ceiling volley, started to stand back in deep court with you, looking at the ceiling, expecting another ceiling return from you.

Strategy: Overhand corner kill

Use an overhead corner kill shot. It's a shot you should practice a lot, for the overhead shot is one of racquetball's most difficult. Drive the ball into the forehand side wall first. The motion is much like a tennis serve. (Diagram 56.)

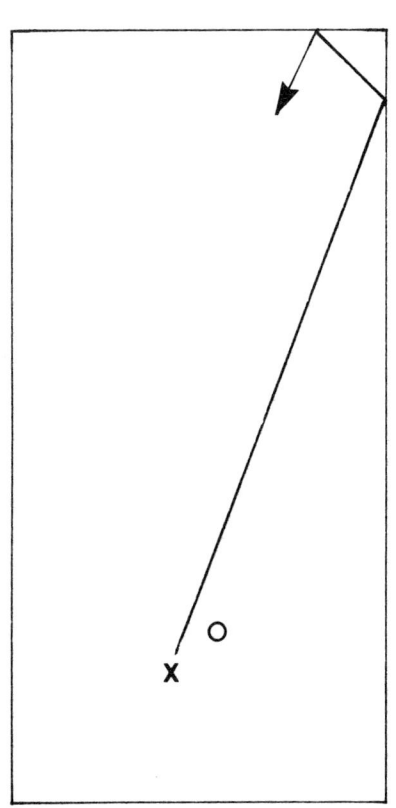

Diagram 56.

Situation: Your opponent has surprised you with an overhead low smash to the corner, but a bit too high for a kill.

Strategy: Re-kill and don't be fooled again

Run forward and try to re-kill the ball, if you can. If not, learn something from the situation: make sure your ceiling shots are good ones that force your opponent to counter with another ceiling shot. If you sense your opponent is going to try an overhead kill, move up to cover the front wall. This will either enable you to get the jump on his kill, or force him to shoot a more defensive ceiling return.

Situation: Your attempt at a pass shot has been badly executed. You are pinned on or near the side wall with the ball between you and center court, and your opponent is running in to shoot.

Strategy: Turn toward the open court

Turn and face the open court, ready for either backhand or forehand shot. Prepare to run in for the pinch or anything else your opponent might hit to the open court. But by all means play safely. Give way, and give your opponent shooting room.

Situation: Your opponent's attempt at a pass shot has left him trapped on the side wall due to the improper execution of the pass attempt.

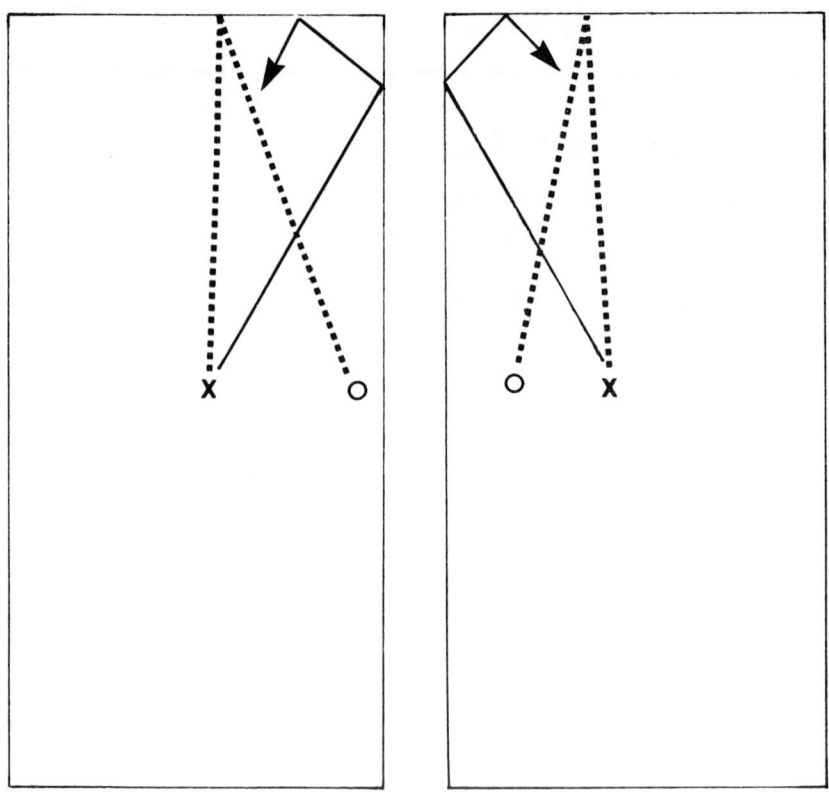

Diagrams 57 and 58.

Strategy: Pinch

Pinch the ball to the side wall he is floundering on. (Diagrams 57 and 58.)

Situation: Your opponent has dived to retrieve the ball.

Jerry Hilecher (diving) is known as the flying retriever on the pro circuit.

Strategy: Don't skip

Since the best place to have your opponent is immobile on the floor, make the most of his or her temporary helplessness. Many players get so excited at seeing their opponent down that they skip the ball into the floor. If your opponent is on the floor behind you, rush forward and kill the ball. (Diagrams 59 and 60.) If your opponent is on the floor in front of you, drive the ball into the front wall so that it rebounds past your opponent and catches a side wall as quickly as possible. (Diagrams 61 and 62.)

Rules of thumb to remember when your opponent is on the floor:
 1. Do not skip the ball.
 2. Do not shoot a ceiling ball; this just gives him time to get up off the floor and retrieve it.
 3. Kill the ball or pass with a low, hard, driving pass.

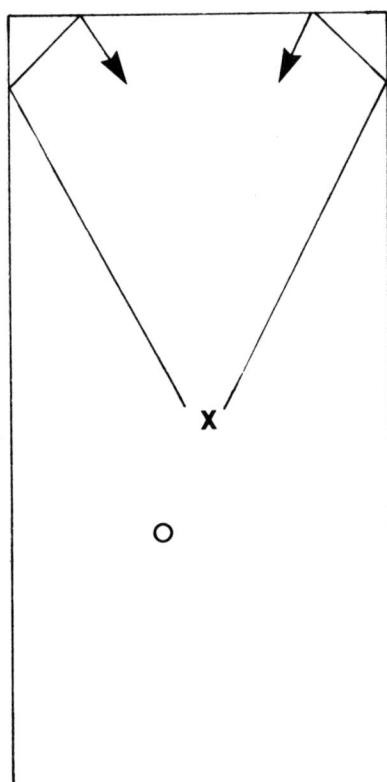
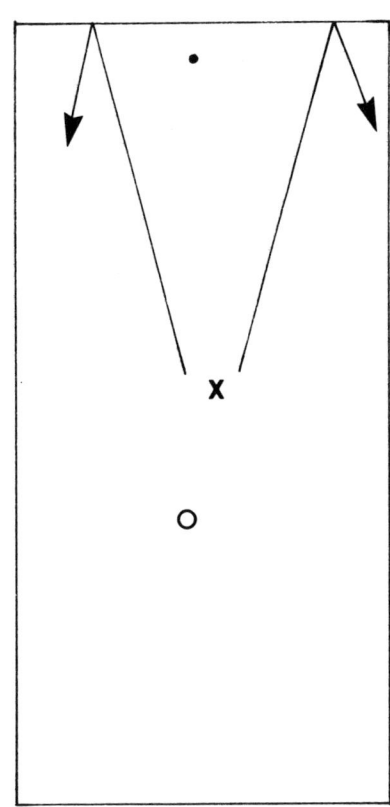

Diagrams 59 and 60. Opponent dives behind you.

Diagrams 61 and 62. Opponent dives in front of you.

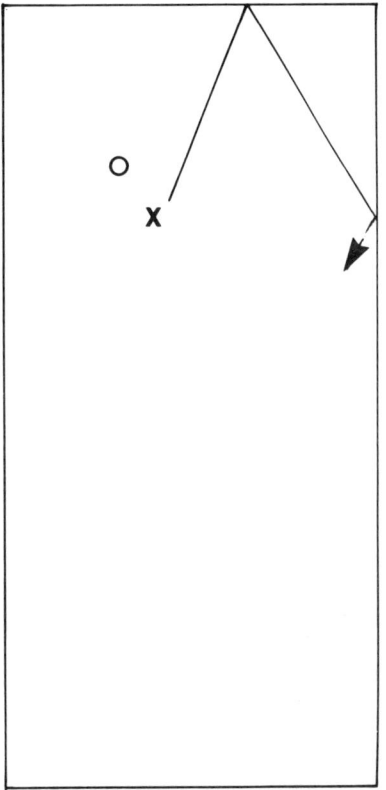

Situation: You've taken a dive to retrieve the ball.

Jerry Hilecher dives to retrieve and kill against Ben Koltun, but the wear and tear of diving makes it inadvisable.

"Killer Dog" Hogan is forced to the air by Hilecher.

Strategy: Kill

Go for the kill. You are in no position to retrieve the ball if you leave it bobbing up high.

It's also a good idea to make sure the dive is necessary. Needless diving is a waste of time and can jeopardize your racquetball career or your head. Use the following guidelines before you dive full out onto the floor.

When diving is worth the risk;
1. The tie breaker.
2. The second game, near the end. You've lost the first game and the score is close.
3. If you're losing and the score is close at the end of game one.

Remember: the sooner you start diving in a match the more likely you are to keep on diving, thereby increasing the risk of injury and decreasing your effectiveness on your feet.

The worst times to dive:
1. The first few points of game one.
2. When you're ahead and easily winning a match.
3. When you are losing the first game by a wide margin.

Other negative notes on diving:
1. You risk injuring yourself.
2. It prevents development of good footwork in the court.
3. Once you start, you tend to dive more often and retrieve less. A person who rarely dives usually has a better retrieval percentage.
4. Diving can cause an avoidable hinder, particularly if the ball comes up at you and you fail to move.

Generally, diving for anyone but the pros should be saved for the match.

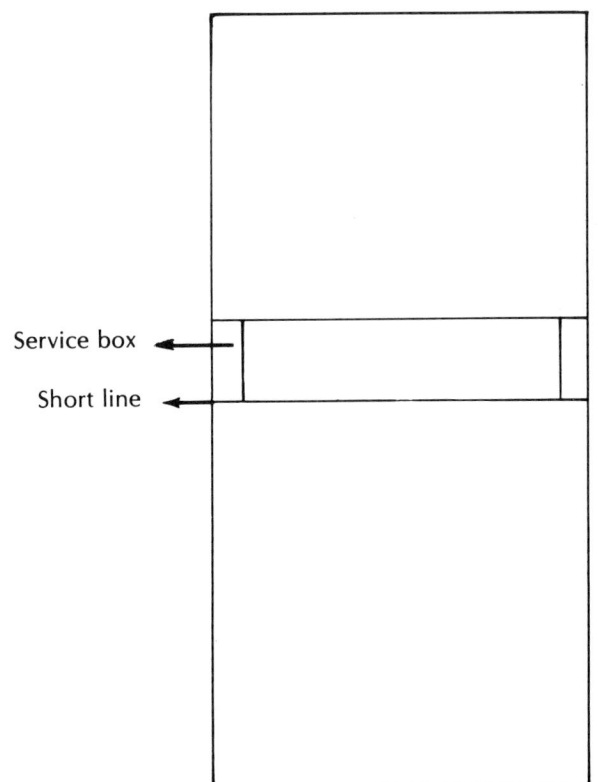

Diagrams 63 and 64.

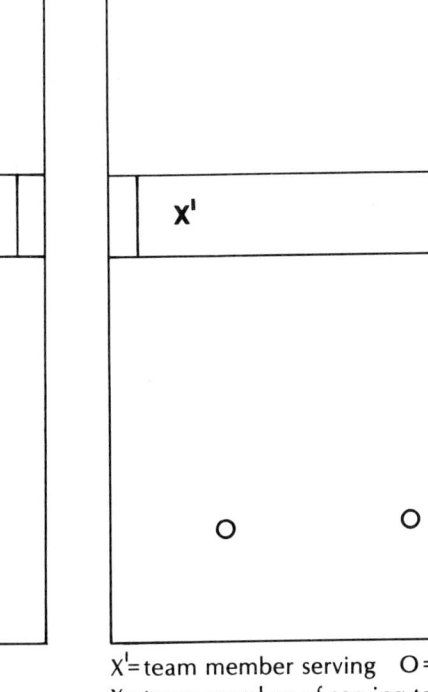

X^I = team member serving   O = receiving team members
X = team member of serving team not yet serving the ball

U.S. Racquetball Association official Chuck Leve rewards perennial Golden Masters champions, Jimmy DiVito and Sam Rizzio, for winning the nationals at the Sports Illustrated Club near Detroit. DeVito and Rizzio, both over sixty, and sporting ample bellies, prove that strategy usually triumphs over condition. Art Payne and Brud Turner, right, were in better shape—to no avail!

Doubles rule summary

In general, the rules for racquetball doubles are the same as racquetball singles with the following considerations:

Serve:

1. The team that serves first gets one serve by one server until it loses its first volley. A side-out results. After that:

2. Each team has two servers. When the rally is lost with the first server, "one down" is called and the second server serves until the rally is lost again. Then a side-out is called and the other team serves.

3. Only the team serving makes points from winning rallies.

4. Your team must serve in the same order every time you are up to serve.

5. You may change the serving order only after a game has been completed.

6. When one member of a team is serving, the other member must stand in the service box until the ball has crossed the short line.

7. The first team to make 21 points wins the game; a team may win with a score of 21-20.

Receive:

1. Either member of the team receiving may return the serve.

2. There is no order in receiving the serve. (This means that the same person may receive every serve for his/her team, although this is highly unlikely.)

Rally:

1. The only hitting order during a rally is between teams, not players. A member of team one hits a ball, a member of team two returns the shot, etc., until the rally is lost (one member of a team fails to return the ball, skips the ball or allows the ball to bounce twice).

Suggestions: Because there are so many people in the court it is advisable to wear eyeguards when playing doubles.

Situation: Your opposing team's right side player plays too close to the right wall.

Strategy: Hit the ball down the right wall

Drive the ball cross court down that wall and jam your right side opponent into the wall, causing a weak return or no return.

Situation: Your partner on the right is too close to the wall. The opposing team is forcing errors.

Strategy: Encourage your partner away from the wall

When your partner is jammed into the side wall you'll have to cover the whole court for that play and make the best return possible. Immediately after your shot, encourage your partner to play away from the side wall and not become a "wall flower" or, worse, a cowering, ineffective partner.

75

Situation: It's the first time you and your partner have played doubles together.

Strategy: Have a game plan/divide the court

The first thing you must do to function as an effective team is to establish boundaries or territories for each of you to cover. For beginners, it's usually best to divide the court in half lengthwise (Diagram 65); the player whose forehand points to the center of the court should take all shots that come up the middle of the court. More advanced players can divide the court diagonally (Diagram 66), with the stronger player taking the left side.

If one of you has a strong forehand while the other has a strong backhand, you might try dividing up the court on the "L theory" (Diagram 67), putting the forehand player in the right front side, and the backhander in the left side. Or, put a strong front court player in front, and a strong back court player in back (Diagram 68).

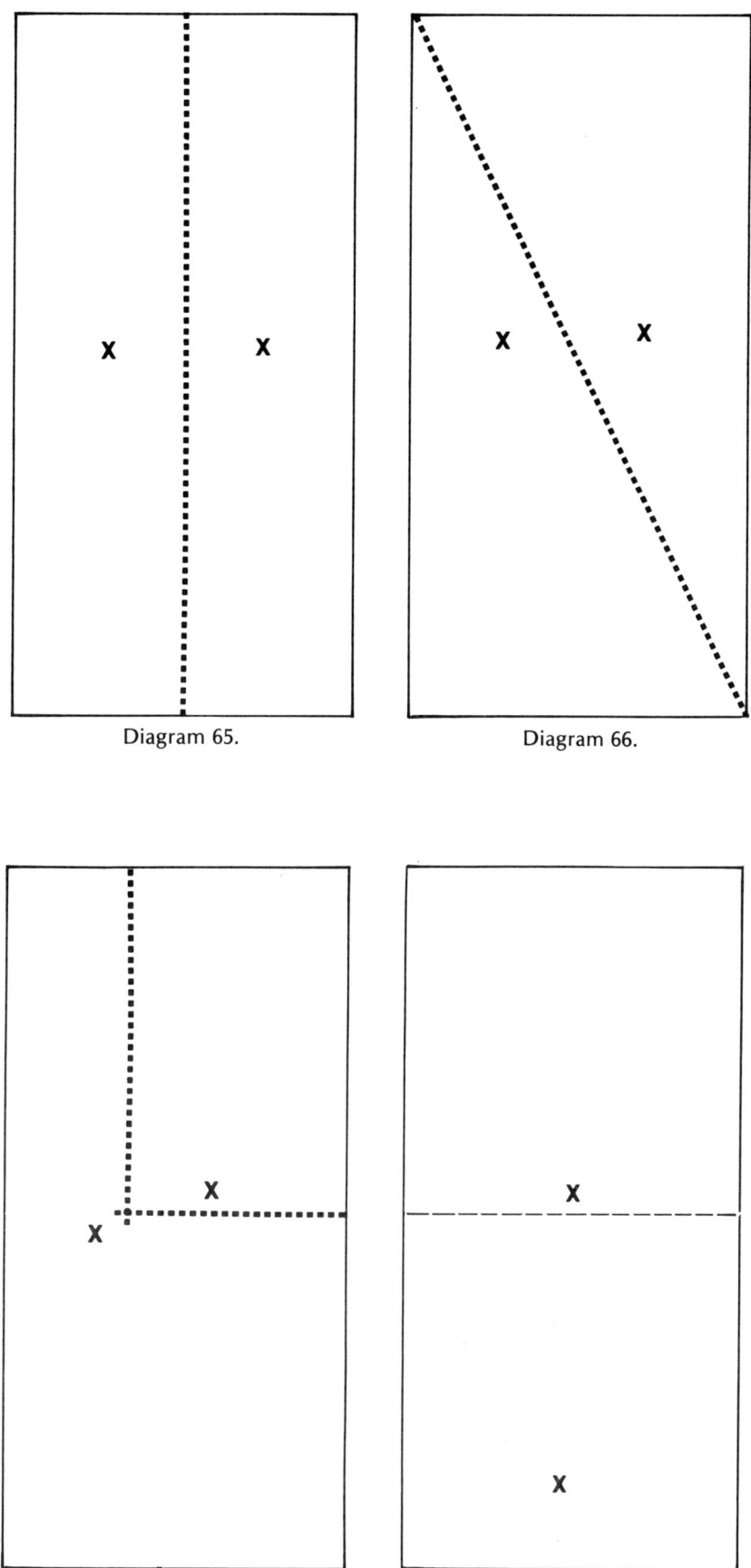

Diagram 65. Diagram 66.

Diagram 67. Diagram 68.

Situation: You are playing the left side and have come to front court to retrieve an attempted forehand corner kill by your right side opponent. Both your opponents are in center court position ready to retrieve your re-kill if the ball should come up.

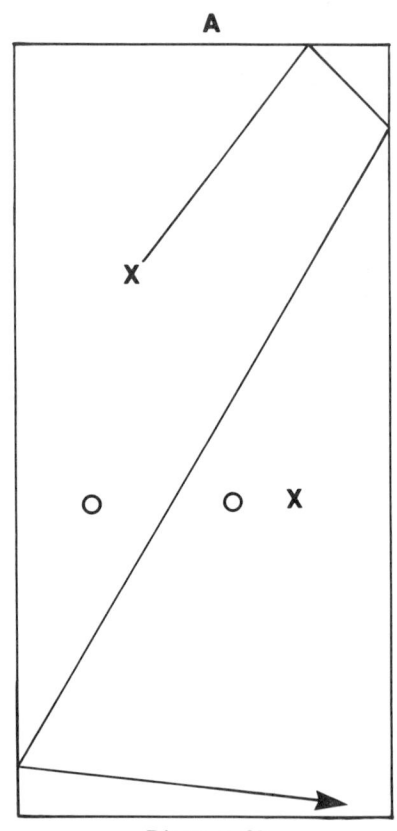

Diagram 69.

Strategy: Shoot a Z ball

Shoot a Z ball. This will immobilize the right side play, and possibly score a point by causing confusion in the enemy. They were expecting a re-kill, and a surprise ball in the corner can often work in this situation. (Diagram 69.)

Situation: Your left side opponent has shot a Z ball while you and your partner are in front court anticipating the kill.

Strategy: The left side player retrieves the shot

If you are playing the left side you should run back to cover the shot. Your partner stays forward and covers front court. (Diagram 70.)

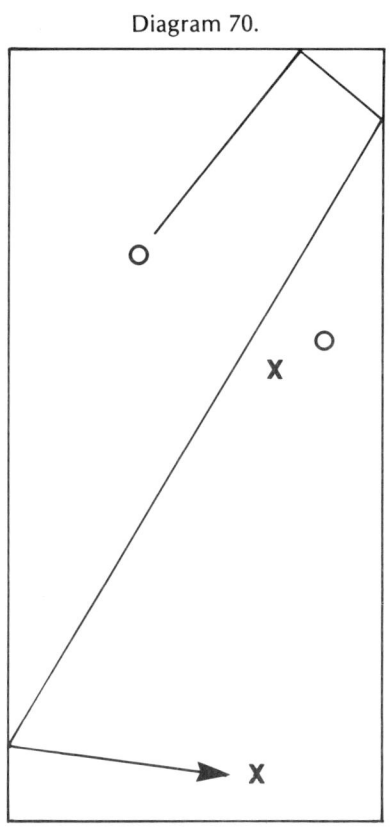

Diagram 70.

Situation: You are playing the right side of the court in doubles, when your opponent on the left side shoots an attempted kill from deep court that pops up to your forehand. You now have a set-up to your forehand with your left side opponent in deep court and your right side opponent up in front court with you.

Strategy: Pinch to the forehand corner

Use a side-wall-front-wall pinch to the forehand corner for a point. (Diagram 71.)

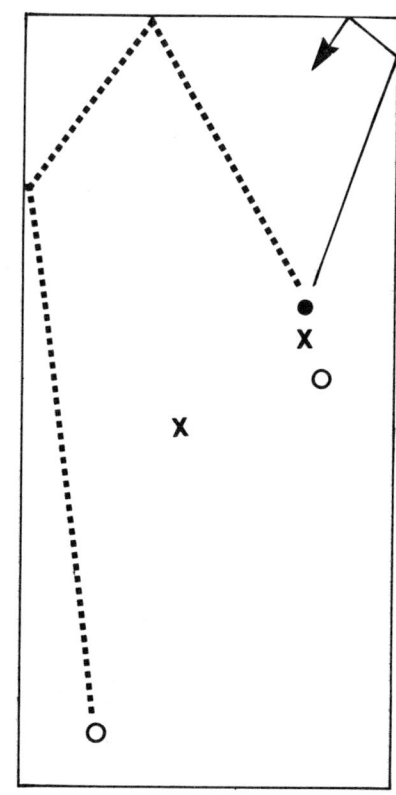

Diagram 71.

Situation: You've attempted to corner-pinch the ball from deep court from the left side. The ball has come up too high, and your right side opponent now has a set-up.

Strategy: Use teamwork to cover the shot

To cover this situation use teamwork. You should immediately run forward to cover a corner pinch attempt. Your right side partner should stay back to cover deep court, should the right side shooter attempt to pass the ball down the wall or cross-court, instead of pinching it. (Diagram 72.)

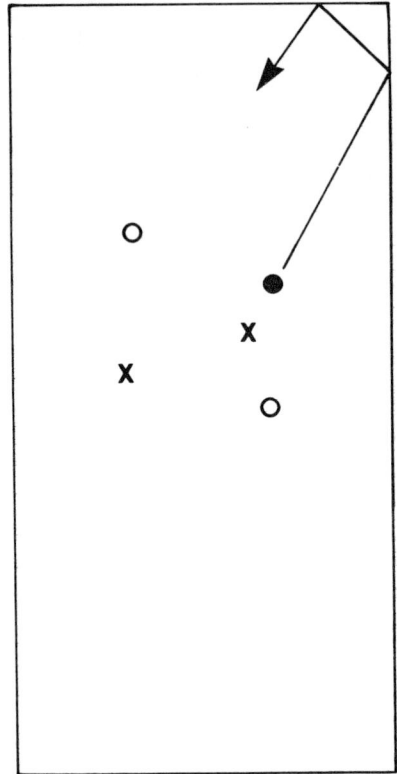

Diagram 72.

Glossary

Ace: Legal serve that eludes the receiver. One point is scored.

Apex: Highest point in a bounce.

Around-the-wall-ball: Shot that hits first the side wall, then the front wall, rebounding to the side from which it was originally struck.

Around-the-wall return: An around-the-wall ball used as a return of service.

Avoidable hinder: Avoidable interference, not necessarily intentional, by one player with another's clear shot. Penalty is loss of serve or point.

Back court: Court area behind the short line.

Backhand: Fundamental stroke hit across your body, starting on the side opposite the hand with which you play. (A right-hander's backhander stroke is from left to right across his body.)

Backhand corner: That area of the court where the side wall and back wall meet; the same side as the player's backhand.

Backhand grip: The position of the hand on the racquet when stroking the backhand.

Backswing: The first step in any stroke, consisting of bringing the racquet into a ready position.

Back wall: The rear wall.

Back wall shot: Shot made from rebound off the rear wall.

Block: A maneuver executed to prevent your opponent from viewing the ball (also called a screen).

Bottom spin: Rotation of the ball in a counterclockwise direction.

Buildups: Conditioning exercises consisting of gradual jog to sprint and back to jog.

Bumper guard: Protective covering on the rim of the racquet head.

Ceiling ball: Ball that hits first the ceiling, then the front wall (or reverse), rebounding to deep court.

Ceiling return: A ceiling ball used as a service return.

Ceiling serve: A serve that hits the ceiling after hitting the front wall. This is illegal and results in a fault.

Center court control: Maintaining position in center court, and forcing your opponent to retrieve in deep court.

Change-of-pace shot: Any shot hit softer than normal.

Club play: Informal competition at local facilities.

Control: The ability to hit the ball to an intended spot.

Corner shot: Any shot that hits at or near the front right or front left corner.

Court hinder: Interference by an obstacle that deflects ball (a light fixture, latch, etc.); point is replayed.

Cross-court drive return: A relatively hard-hit service return that hits the front wall and passes the server on the side opposite that from which the shot came.

Cross-court pass shot: A cross-court pass hit during play. *See also* cross-court serve.

Crotch: A juncture of two playing surfaces.

Crotch serve: Serve that strikes the juncture of the front wall and the floor or ceiling; illegal.

Crowding: Playing so close to your opponent that you hamper his swing or his shot selection.

Cutthroat: Game with three players with each server during his turn playing against the other two players.

Dead ball: Any ball out of play; a racquetball that does not bounce as high as normal, also a ball that breaks during play.

Defensive shot: A return shot usually made to continue the rally rather than to end it.

Die: A ball that barely reaches the front wall

and rebounds with little or no bounce is said to die.

Dig: To retrieve a low shot before it strikes the floor twice.

Doubles: Game of two teams of two players each.

Down-the-line pass shot: A shot hit from near a side wall directly to the front wall and rebounds back along that same side wall.

Drive return: A relatively hard-hit service return striking only the front wall.

Drive serve: A relatively hard-hit serve that strikes the front wall and rebounds in a straight line to deep court.

Drop shot: A soft-hit ball aimed low into the front wall from front court.

Error: Failure to return an apparently playable ball.

Exchange: *See* rally.

Fault: Illegal serve or other infraction of serving rules.

Flat roll-out: A perfect kill shot: the ball hits the front wall so close to the floor that it rebounds with no bounce.

Float: A ball that travels upward so slowly that your opponent has enough time to set up for his next shot.

Fly shot: a ball played on rebound from front wall before it hits floor.

Follow-through: The completion of your swing after contact with the ball.

Foot fault: Illegal placement of your foot outside the service zone during serve.

Footwork: How your feet move in relationship to the rest of your body, the ball, and the racquet.

Forehand: Fundamental stroke hit across your body from the same side as the hand with which you play. (A right-handed player's forehand stroke is from right to left across his body.

Front court: Area in front of the short line.

Front line: *See* service line.

Front-wall-first ceiling ball: A shot that strikes first the front wall, then the ceiling.

Front-wall-first ceiling return: A ceiling ball return of service that strikes first the front wall, then the ceiling, rebounding to deep court.

Front wall-side wall kill: A kill shot that hits first the front wall, then the side wall. *See also* kill.

Game: Twenty-one points.

Garfinkel serve: A forehand cross-court serve to an opponent's forehand.

Grip: The manner in which the racquet is held.

Half-and-half: Definition of court responsibilities in doubles: an imaginary line is drawn down the middle of the court.

Hand-out: Loss of serve by first partner serving for his team in doubles. *See also* Side-out.

Handshake grip: Method of holding racquet in handshake manner.

Head: Hitting surface of the racquet; the face.

I formation: Definition of court responsibilities in doubles: one player plays front court, and his partner plays back court.

IRA: International Racquetball Association, the governing body of racquetball.

Inning: A complete round of play in which both sides serve.

Isolation strategy: The hitting of several consecutive shots to one player in doubles and very few to his partner.

Kill: Shot that hits the front wall and rebounds too close to the floor to be returned.

Live ball: Any ball in play: a racquetball with a high bounce.

Lob ball: A high soft-hit shot.

Lob return: A high, soft return of service.

Lob serve: A high, soft service.

Long serve: Any serve that rebounds to the

back wall before it strikes the floor.

Masters: In singles competition for players over 40; in doubles competition, one player must be at least 40, and his partner, at least 45.

Nonfront serve: A serve that hits any surface other than the front wall before hitting the front wall. This serve is illegal, and the penalty is loss of service.

Off-speed drive: A drive shot hit at medium speed, used for change of pace.

Off-the-back-wall kill: A kill shot struck as the ball rebounds off the back wall. *See also* kill.

Offensive position: Approximately center court; the most desirable spot for offensive play.

Offensive shot: Shot designed to win rally.

One-on-two: Game with three players in which the server plays the other two for the entirety of the game.

Opened: Racquet head faces a side wall rather than the front wall.

Out: Loss of serve as a result of an illegal serve.

Overhead: A shot that is struck over your head.

Pass shot: Ball shot out of your opponent's reach.

Pinch shot: A low shot that hits a side wall before it hits the front wall.

Point: Unit of scoring; tally scored by a successful player. Only the server can score a point.

Point of contact: The exact spot at which the racquet strikes the ball.

Rally: The time during which the ball is kept in play.

Ready position: The stance taken as you wait for the serve.

Receiver: The person to whom the serve is hit.

Receiving line: That line five feet in back of the short line. The receiver may not cross the receiving line umil the ball has crossed the short line.

Referee: The person who makes all judgment calls in tournament play.

Reverse cross-court serve: *See* Garfinkel serve.

Roadrunner: A player whose specialty is retrieving.

Safety hinder: Stoppage of play when further play could result in injury.

Seamco 558: The official ball for the game of racquetball. The standard ball is 2½ inches in diameter, weighs approximately 1.4 ounces, and, at 76°F., will bounce 67-72 inches high when dropped from a height of 100 inches.

Serve: The act of putting the ball in play.

Server: Player who puts the ball in play.

Serve return: The receiver's first shot after the ball has been served.

Service box: The area 18 inches from the side wall, in which the nonserving member of a doubles team stands with his back to the wall while his partner serves.

Service line: The line parallel to and 5 feet in front of the short line.

Service zone: The court area between the short line and the service line, in which the server must stand while serving.

Set-up: A shot that is easily returned.

Shooters: Players who depend to a great degree on kill shots. *See also* kill.

Short line: Line halfway between and parallel to the front and back walls.

Short serve: Serve that contacts the front wall first but fails to rebound beyond the short line. This serve is illegal, and two such serves in succession result in loss of service.

Side wall-front wall kill: A kill shot that hits the side wall and rebounds to the front wall. *See also* Pinch.

Side-out: Loss of serve.

Singles: Game of two players, one against the other.
Skip ball: Ball that hits the floor before it reaches the front wall.
Skip-in: *See* skip ball.
Straight kill: A kill shot hit directly into the front wall. *See also* kill.
Thong: Strap attached to racquet and worn around player's wrist. The strap must be fastened securely in order to eliminate the possibility of the racquet's flying out of control.
Three-quarters one-quarter: Definition of court responsibilities in doubles: an imaginary line is drawn diagonally from one front corner to the opposite back corner.
Three-quarter speed drive: *See* off-speed drive.
Three-wall serve: Serve that hits three walls on fly; illegal.
Top spin: Rotation of the ball in a clockwise direction.
Trigger grip: Method of holding racquet as if it were a pistol.
Tournament play: Formal competitive play under scheduled conditions.
Turning point: The time during a game or match that is considered crucial.
Unavoidable hinder: Accidental interference with opponent or flight of ball. No penalty is suffered, and the rally is replayed.
Undercut: To put backspin on the ball.
Volley: To hit the ball on a fly.
V pass shot: Passing shot in which the ball strikes first the front wall, then the side wall or near the short line, rebounding in V fashion away from or behind your opponent.
Wallpaper ball: A shot that hugs so close to a wall that it is extremely difficult to return.
Winners: Kill shots. *See also* kill.
Z ball: Shot that hits the front wall, the side wall, and then the opposite wall without striking the floor.
Z ball return: Z ball used as return of service.
Z serve: *See* cross-court serve.

Index

B

Bertolucci, Dan, vii
Brin, Bill, v, viii
Brumfield, Charlie, v, vii, 2, *illus.* 7, 18
Buckun, Tony, *illus.* 27

C

Conditioners for racquetball, 4

D

DeVito, Jimmy, *illus.* 71
Drake, Charlie, v, vii
Drive serve, 20, *illus.* 21

F

Fancher, Terry, viii

G

Garbage serve, 44, *illus.* 46

H

Hilecher, Jerry, v, vii, *illus.* 47, 68, 70
Hogan, Marty, v, vii, viii, 1, 2, *illus.* 7, 47, 50, 70

K

Kendler, Boby, vii
Koltun, Benny, vii, *illus.* 20, 70

L

Leve, Chuck, v, *illus.* 71
Lob serve, 44, *illus.* 44-46
Loveday, Carl, vii
Lynch, John, viii

M

Marriott, Janelle, V

N

National Racquetball, vii
National Racquetball Association, v

P

Payne, Art, *illus.* 71
Pydo, Don, *illus.* 27

R

Rizzio, Sam, *illus.* 71

S

Sauser, Jean, viii, *illus.* 28
Shay, Steve, v
Steding, Peggy, vii
Strandemo, Steve, vii

T

Turner, Bud, *illus.* 71

W

Williams, Kathy, v